Playing and Learning Outdoors

Playing and Learning Outdoors shows early years practitioners how to get the very best from outdoor play and learning for the enjoyment, health and education of all children from ages three to seven years.

Fully updated to reflect the current status and understandings regarding outdoor provision within early childhood education frameworks, and extended to age seven, this new edition will allow practitioners to develop rich and stimulating outdoor play provision in any early years setting and enable them to feel confident to offer wonderful play experiences outdoors.

Playing and Learning Outdoors offers practitioners achievable advice and support, based on approaches which are appropriate and effective for young children's all-round well-being and development. This invaluable resource also includes practical advice on:

- movement and physical play;
- playing with water, sand and other natural materials;
- plants, living things and growing;
- construction, imaginative and creative play.

This second edition also includes a brand new chapter on 'Providing experiences beyond the garden gate', which urges practitioners to harness the huge potential contained in the immediate locality and local community just outside the setting's own boundaries, as an 'additional layer' of their outdoor provision.

Filled with advice and support, this lively, inspiring and accessible book will help practitioners to develop a truly practical and enjoyable approach to learning through play outdoors for all children aged from three to seven.

Jan White works nationally and abroad to advocate and support high-quality outdoor provision for services for children from birth to seven. She is currently an Early Education associate, adviser for several landscape and equipment companies and mentor to Sandfield Natural Play Centre. She also teaches on the Masters programme at CREC (Birmingham City University).

Playing and Learning Outdoors

Making provision for high quality experiences in the outdoor environment with children 3–7

Second edition

Jan White

 Routledge
Taylor & Francis Group

LONDON AND NEW YORK

Second edition published 2014
by Routledge
2 Park Square, Milton Park, Abingdon, Oxon OX14 4RN

and by Routledge
711 Third Avenue, New York, NY 10017

Routledge is an imprint of the Taylor & Francis Group, an informa business

© 2014 Jan White

The right of Jan White to be identified as author of this work has been asserted by her in accordance with sections 77 and 78 of the Copyright, Designs and Patents Act 1988.

First edition published by Routledge 2007

British Library Cataloguing in Publication Data
A catalogue record for this book is available from the British Library

Library of Congress Cataloging in Publication Data
A catalog record for this book has been requested

ISBN: 978-0-415-62314-8 (hbk)
ISBN: 978-0-415-62315-5 (pbk)
ISBN: 978-0-203-10542-9 (ebk)

Typeset in Bembo
by Wearset Ltd, Boldon, Tyne and Wear

Printed and bound by Bell & Bain Ltd, Glasgow

MIX
Paper from
responsible sources
FSC® C007785

This book is dedicated to all the children who have shown me how much the outdoors matters to them, to all those adults who enjoy sharing children's pleasure with being outside and to the growing number of colleagues dedicated to advocating and establishing ample, rich and daily outdoor experience as a right for all children.

Contents

Acknowledgements

I would like to acknowledge the most significant of very many experiences over many years that have built the appreciation and understanding represented in this book.

First, thanks to my parents, Jean and John, for giving me access to such excellent childhood play outdoors and to my siblings, Julie and Phil, for being perfect outdoor playmates.

Big thanks to both Jacqui Fynn and Hill End Camp, and to Christine Goldsack and the Sheffield quality development scheme for giving me such inspirational guidance and experiences. Thanks to Learning through Landscapes for a remarkable three and a half years and to the Vision and Values Partnership, especially Majorie Ouvry, who has been a personal inspiration and hero.

Very special thanks go to all the children who have allowed me to watch them at play outside and to the many educators who have shared their practice with me. Particular thanks to the children and parents who have allowed the use of their photographs: Bents Green Preschool; Bognor Regis Nursery School and Children's Centre; Carol Duffy; Children's Oasis Nurseries, Dubai; Liz Knowles; Liz Magraw and Hind Leys Preschool; Jane Wratten and Slinn Street Starters; Menna Godfrey and Quackers; Sue Scott, Ann Thompson and Sandfield Natural Play Centre; Vanessa Lloyd, Christchurch CP School and St Asaph VP Infant School.

And my biggest thanks go to my own children, Laurie and Bryn (who have now gone out into the world as enthusiastic, capable and self-directed young adults), for allowing me to have such fun reliving my childhood and to learn so much more in the process.

I would also like to thank my publisher, Alison Foyle, and her team for their enthusiasm towards seeing this second edition in print and their patience in waiting for it; and to my husband, Ed, for not only calmly putting up with the chaotic house and timetable but also accommodating all the extra books I have needed to gather for my research.

Introduction

The young child's right to being, playing and learning outdoors

> *A child's world is fresh and new and beautiful, full of wonder and excitement. It is our misfortune that for most of us that clear-eyed vision, that true instinct for what is beautiful and awe-inspiring, is dimmed and even lost before we reach adulthood. If I had influence with the good fairy who is supposed to preside over the christening of all children I should ask that her gift to each child in the world be a sense of wonder so indestructible that it would last throughout life, as an unfailing antidote against the boredom and disenchantments of later years, the sterile preoccupation with things that are artificial, the alienation from the sources of our strength.*
>
> (Rachel Carson, *The Sense of Wonder*, first published in 1956)

The *Shared Vision and Values for Outdoor Provision in the Early Years* (Vision and Values Partnership 2004) states:

- All children have the right to experience and enjoy the essential and special nature of being outdoors.
- Young children thrive and their minds and bodies develop best when they have free access to stimulating outdoor environments for learning through play and real experiences.
- Knowledgeable and enthusiastic adults are crucial to unlocking the potential of outdoors.

Young children have rights:

- to explore what matters to them and what they are biologically designed and driven to do;
- to experience things, events and ideas in active, multi-sensory and multi-layered ways that enable them to think and understand at an embodied level;
- to flourish from the deep well-being that being outside and in nature provide;
- to be in an environment that naturally includes them through its diversity and flexibility;
- to interact on an even and egalitarian level with other children and the adults who are living and learning with them.

In short, they have an abiding need and a human right to be outdoors.

Young children need outdoor play. When given the choice, the outdoors is where most children want to be and play outdoors is what they most want. In several surveys carried out over recent years, including those carried out to inform the development of the *Early Years Foundation Stage* in England and the *Foundation Phase* in Wales, the outdoors always comes out at the top of children's priorities and favourite things in their early childhood education setting. Parents too value it highly and are aware that early years provision gives their child access to experiences outdoors that they do not otherwise get enough of. As we move in the countries of the UK and Ireland towards an understanding that experiential and playful learning is the most appropriate and effective approach for education up to the age of seven (in particular, in recent Welsh, Scottish and Irish curriculum developments), the crucial role of the outdoors in supporting children to thrive and develop is increasingly foregrounded. This new edition of *Playing and Learning Outdoors* seeks to support all educators working with children from three to seven years, drawing strongly from both long-established practice in early childhood education and emerging understandings about how young brains and bodies develop best.

Throughout our long history, humans have been immersed in the outdoors, living and working as social groups to find what we needed to survive and thrive. As a result, our bodies and minds have been shaped and honed by all the complexities of the natural world. As adults, we benefit greatly from being outside in fresh air and in contact with nature. However, it is imperative that, from birth, young children spend considerable amounts of time outdoors, bathed in the richness of this fascinating and complex environment. The outdoors holds an enormous amount of potential to support healthy and complete emotional, physical, social and cognitive development. Indoor environments just cannot reach the richness and relevance of experience that full development requires. Young children love being outdoors: they are designed to be outside and their bodies and minds need them to be there. They need *us* to have a deep and comprehensive understanding of this. They rely on us to be committed to providing as much time outside as possible, every single day, throughout the year. They thrive when we are enthusiastic too, taking pleasure in being outdoors together with them.

Young children have a particular way of interacting with their world and of learning about and from it. They interact and learn through movement and doing, involving their whole body and using it to find out and to express. They take in information through all their senses, with less emphasis on talk than we do as adults. Their brains are like sponges, noticing detail and things that adults miss or filter out. They need real and relevant experiences, with lots of handling, direct contact and playful exploration of materials. They also need lots of opportunities to imitate, repeat and revisit through their own self-directed play. Learning is most successful when children share experiences with adults and especially with other children. These are all factors we should aim to build into any learning opportunity we provide, whether inside or outside, but the outdoors can be especially effective at offering children experiences in the ways best suited to them.

Play outdoors offers children:

- access to space with opportunities to be their natural, exuberant physical and noisy selves;
- fresh air and direct experience of how the elements of the weather feel;
- contact with natural and living things, to maintain their inborn affinity, curiosity and fascination with all things belonging to the natural world;
- freedom to be inquisitive, exploratory, adventurous, innovative and messy;
- a vast range of real experiences that are relevant and meaningful and that make sense;
- endless opportunities for discovery, play and talk so that new experiences can be processed, understood and used;
- an environment that feeds information into all the senses at the same time;
- involvement with the whole body, giving deeply felt meanings and all-round physical health;
- movement experiences that develop essential structures within the brain and nervous system;
- emotional and mental well-being, where self-image and esteem grow;
- social interactions that build relationships, social skills and enjoyment of being with others;
- lots of opportunities to set themselves challenges and to learn how to keep themselves safe;
- a place that meets the way they learn best and allows them to express feelings, thoughts and ideas in a way more suited to them.

The outdoors offers a perfect companion to provision indoors, working in harmony and providing a complementary environment that enhances and extends what we are able to give children inside. In thinking about outdoor provision, the central idea that we must hold in our minds is that the outdoors is *different* to the indoors; that is why it is necessary in early years provision that is successful in meeting young children's needs. We need to be very clear about *how* the outdoors differs from the indoors, *why* children benefit from being outside and *why* the outdoors is such a good place for young children's development and learning. Recognising the differences gives us a crystal-clear rationale for putting as much effort into provision and planning for the outdoors as well as the indoors. Just as importantly, this gives us the key for *what* to provide and *how* to plan for the outdoor half of our environment. Knowing what makes the outdoor special and unique provides us with a set of guidelines for making decisions about provision, planning and interacting with children.

In our efforts to develop outdoor learning, there is a danger of taking away or losing what is unique and special for children about the outdoors. Learning outdoors is certainly not about taking the indoors out, nor should we take the teacher role outside. This is the child's domain, a more democratic place for learning about the world and about being human, where relationships and meanings with people, places and things are explored and developed *by the child*. It is important that we retain the characteristics that make the outdoors different and special for children. The beach and the woodland are the ultimate learning environments for young children. What are the elements and characteristics that make these such marvellous places? How can we capture their key elements and characteristics, and make them appropriately available and provocative in our own outdoor spaces? If we strive to create their variety and flexibility, we can gradually provide an environment that children can manipulate, change and control, making them the author of their own investigations and play, and the architect of their own body and brain. It is becoming clear that we need to return to thinking of our outdoor spaces as *gardens*, rather than playgrounds or playspaces; in which children explore and play, learn through actions and feeling, and develop their incredible capacities for imagination, creation and logical thinking. Above all, a sense of attachment and belonging to our world is vital for children's deep well-being, and for the future well-being of our beautiful, wonderful, fascinating and nurturing Earth. For further thinking on the special nature of the outdoors, see my chapter in *Outdoor Provision in the Early Years* (White, Sage Publications 2011, chapter 5).

It is important that adults working with young children spend time thinking carefully about the nature of outdoor experiences. Over the last decade, we have moved a long way forward with a returning commitment to harnessing the outdoors for playing, well-being and learning. However, so many practitioners are still working with difficult environments that were not purpose-built or designed with good knowledge of what children and adults need. Successful outdoor play and learning requires as much thought, preparation and planning as provision receives indoors, and there is a great deal to it. Achieving effective provision is a slow process that must be done with care and reflection, in manageable bite-sized chunks. It is vital to make a start, but best not to rush ahead! Developing outdoor provision and practice is a long-term and multi-faceted process, which requires an extensive literature to support thinking in all its various aspects, just as we have for thinking about environments, provision and practice indoors. It is of course not at all possible to cover everything about outdoor provision in one single volume, and since the first edition of this book, the interest and commitment to high-quality outdoor play has continued to grow such that many useful and inspiring texts have been published, each with its own focus and value for practitioners. In the *further resources and support* section given at the end of this chapter, I have given a short outline as to the focus of each book and in what way it might prove useful. There are still gaps (such as focused work on engaging parents) and many questions remain for research into young children's outdoor play. I hope that further publications will begin to fill these gaps and that authors will continue to think about, discuss and stretch our understandings about being, playing and learning outdoors. I have also been able to greatly enhance the further information and resources lists for each ingredient. While I am aware that this book is read beyond Britain, I have focused on what is available in the UK — however, it is likely that equivalent resources exist in each part of the world.

Any good recipe consists of wholesome ingredients that blend well together to make a tasty and healthy meal, with expectations about the quality of these ingredients and clear instructions for preparation that draw from tested and trusted techniques. Having spent many years concentrating on provision and practice for outdoor play, I believe there are six major ingredients that make up a full menu for rich and satisfying on-site outdoor provision for young children. I have therefore given a chapter to exploring how each ingredient can best be provided: water, natural materials, growing and the living world, movement and physical play, imagination and creativity, and construction (including den play). It has also become clear to me that a seventh vital ingredient should be added by harnessing the wonderful places, experiences, people, creatures and events that exist in the immediate surroundings of the setting — the locality and community just outside its boundaries. Including these as an additional layer of the everyday outdoor provision captures important experiential learning potential that just cannot be offered on site — however, this ingredient is currently severely underused. I have therefore added a new chapter in this second edition regarding providing outdoor experiences beyond the garden, and I urge readers to positively consider this highly valuable aspect of practice. Each of these ingredients offers highly holistic learning experiences that contribute to all areas of development and learning. Whatever way your curriculum categorises areas of learning, you will see how each ingredient covers them all in the holistic way young children need their learning diet.

In order to offer a complete environment for well-being and learning, we need to offer all seven ingredients to some degree, but it is possible to start off small with something manageable in each aspect and to gradually develop as confidence and understanding grow. Although the chapters are organised under these main aspects of provision, it is difficult to put provision neatly into boxes and you will find that each interacts and overlaps with most of the others. So, although each chapter stands alone to some extent, you will find more by cross-referencing between them. As an example, dance is an activity that is both physical and creative and there is complementary discussion in both chapters.

For each ingredient of outdoor provision, chapters are organised broadly into:

*   why this is a main ingredient and what it offers children;
*   how to make provision for this ingredient, with suggestions for good resources;
*   making the most of this element of provision;
*   lists of children's books and rhymes that support the theme;
*   sources of further information and resources.

In this second edition, I have been able to add extensively to the lists of relevant children's books. All references were available on Amazon at the time of writing; however, many are old or second-hand. Although children's picture books can quickly go out of print, the Internet now enables us to purchase used books at very low prices and this saves a great deal of money or allows settings to provide good selections at much less cost, whilst embedding the ethic of sustainability in children's minds. Books more suited to the older end of the age group covered by this book are marked with an asterisk.

Just as all good ingredients in a really good recipe have been carefully selected, grown in the best conditions and prepared with reference to the best techniques, another set of themes concerning effective early years practice and how this applies to children's play outdoors weaves throughout the book. Since it would be repetitive to explore each of these for each ingredient, where appropriate I have selected one chapter to go into a particular theme in greater depth, but each theme applies just as much to every ingredient. These themes can be summarised as:

- development and learning taking place through a mix of real experience and exploration balanced with lots of play;
- working from children's natural interests and motivations as effective provision is child-led;
- direct and hands-on access to the real physical world and the real human world as the most relevant, motivational and meaningful learning contexts and content for the developing child;
- setting up continuous provision to enable children to self-select and direct their own learning;
- storage, containment and organisation as key factors needing careful thought and attention;
- emergent, flexible planning allowing adjustment to make best use of opportunities and spontaneity;
- slowing down to the child's pace, practising 'slowliness' and making the most of each and every detail of an experience, according to children's interest and attention;
- allowing children plenty of time to explore, play, return, repeat and 'wallow' so that they can get really deeply involved, as essential for effective and satisfying learning;
- engaging parents and carers in what their child is getting from play outdoors, and learning from what they know about their child;
- planning based on on-going observation, formative assessment and thoughtful evaluation outdoors: the 'notice–recognise–respond' cycle, or 'what?–so what?–now what?' (Claire Devlin, personal communication, 2012);
- each element of provision offering holistic experiences with contributions to each area of learning;
- each ingredient of outdoor provision being available in some form in most or all parts of the outdoor space;

- the adult role as thoughtful, complex, skilled and sensitively managed;
- challenge as vital for learning and development, appreciation of the benefits of an experience and managing risks for both safety and opportunity (benefit–risk assessment);
- achieving inclusion by meeting each and every child's needs as an individual.

I have not had space to adequately deal with such other important issues as the organisation of the transition area between indoors and outside and the role a specific policy for outdoor provision can play in its management. For a closer look at inclusion for children with disability and special needs, I recommend Theresa Casey's book *Inclusive Play* (2010). For more on risk assessment and management, read *Too Safe for Their Own Good?* by Jennie Lindon (2011) and refer to the Health and Safety Executive's website, www.hse.gov.uk. I also recommend specific benefit–risk assessment training and identification of a staff member with dedicated responsibility for ensuring adequate risk management procedures are in place and followed at all times (especially through staff induction and supervision). For on-going inspiration and support for developing outdoor play provision, I strongly recommend that you join Learning through Landscape's membership support scheme, *Early Years Outdoors*.

Other books deal with design and planning of outdoor spaces. I would advise, however, not to over-plan or designate your outdoor spaces and not to split your space into too many subject-specific 'areas'. A basic level of structure in the environment is important for young children and simple zoning can be very useful, provided the space remains flexible and dynamic, and elements of provision are not segregated or limited to specific places. For example, there is no reason why plants, even those for food production, should not be integrated throughout the outdoor space so that children have close, meaningful contact with the natural world as much as possible; and action and movement can and should happen almost everywhere. Your unique arrangement of where and how you offer the main ingredients will depend on your own space and priorities. For further thinking on the characteristics of a powerful outdoor environment for young children, see chapter 3 in *Exploring Outdoor Play in the Early Years* (Maynard and Waters, Open University Press 2014).

Because you are using everyday and natural materials, you need to pay close attention to whether they present a hazard in the context they will be used and for the individual children you are working with. As in every aspect of early years provision, children's safety is paramount, and it is the setting's responsibility to ensure that all experiences, whether indoors or outdoors and whether deriving from the contents of this book or from elsewhere, are free from undue or extreme levels of risk of harm. The author and the publishers have made every attempt to draw the reader's attention to possibilities of harm and to sensible and effective benefit–risk-assessment and management procedures, but this cannot be achieved without active and diligent commitment by practitioners using this book. The author and publishers disclaim responsibility for how the ideas and suggestions in this book are applied in settings with children.

Everything in this book is underpinned by the thinking and words in the *Shared Vision and Values for Outdoor Provision in the Early Years*, as produced by the Vision and Values Partnership and reproduced in full below. My aim with this book is to help you to create outdoor play provision in which your young children will thrive. With a clear vision of what you want for your children that gives a good sense of direction, a positive attitude to overcome any difficulties and the readiness to make a start, however small, the journey will begin. I very much like the mantra I heard from school grounds developer Sharon Danks in the USA: 'Think big; take small steps; never give up!' Once started, it can be a most enjoyable journey, and one that is vitally important for every young child.

I would like to leave you with more wise and highly appropriate words by Rachel Carson, written in 1956 and re-published in the beautiful book *The Sense of Wonder* in 1998:

> It is not half so important to know as to feel. If facts are the seeds that later produce knowledge and wisdom, then the emotions and impressions of the senses are the fertile soil in which the seeds must grow. The years of early childhood are the time to prepare the soil.... It is more important to pave the way for the child to want to know than to put him on a diet of facts he is not ready to assimilate.

Core values for high-quality outdoor experiences for young children

1 *Young children should be outdoors as much as indoors and need a well-designed, well-organised, integrated indoor–outdoor environment, preferably with indoors and outdoors available simultaneously.*
Outdoor provision is an essential part of the child's daily environment and life, not an option or an extra. Each half of the indoor–outdoor environment offers significantly different, but complementary, experiences and ways of being to young children. They should be available simultaneously and be experienced in a joined-up way, with each being given equal status and attention for their contribution to young children's well-being, health, stimulation and all areas of development.

Outdoor space must be considered a necessary part of an early years environment, be well thought through and well organised to maximise its value and usability by children and adults, and design and planning must support developmentally appropriate practice, being driven by children's interests and needs.

2 *Play is the most important activity for young children outside.*
Play is the means through which children find stimulation, well-being and happiness, and is the means through which they grow physically, intellectually and

emotionally. Play is the most important thing for children to do outside and the most relevant way of offering learning outdoors. The outdoor environment is very well suited to meeting children's needs for all types of play, building upon first-hand experiences.

3 *Outdoor provision can, and must, offer young children experiences which have a lot of meaning to them and are led by the child.*
Because of the freedom the outdoors offers to move on a large scale, to be active, noisy and messy and to use all their senses with their whole body, young children engage in the way they most need to explore, make sense of life and express their feelings and ideas. Many young children relate much more strongly to learning offered outdoors rather than indoors.

All areas of learning must be offered through a wide range of holistic experiences, both active and calm, which make the most of what the outdoors has to offer.

Outdoor provision needs to be organised so that children are stimulated, and able, to follow their own interests and needs through play-based activity, giving them independence, self-organisation, participation and empowerment. The adult role is crucial in achieving this effectively.

4 *Young children need all the adults around them to understand why outdoor play provision is essential for them, and adults who are committed and able to make its potential available to them.*
Young children need practitioners who value and enjoy the outdoors themselves, see the potential and consequences it has for young children's well-being and development, and want to be outside with them. Attitude, understanding, commitment and positive thinking are important, as well as the skills to make the best use of what the outdoors has to offer and to effectively support child-led learning; the adult role outdoors must be as deeply considered as that indoors. Practitioners must be able to recognise, capture and share children's learning outdoors with parents and other people working with the child, so that they too become enthused. Cultural differences in attitude to the outdoors need to be understood and worked with sensitively to reach the best outcomes for children.

5 *The outdoor space and curriculum must harness the special nature of the outdoors, to offer children what the indoors cannot. This should be the focus for outdoor provision, complementing and extending provision indoors.*
The outdoors offers young children essential experiences vital to their well-being, health and development in all areas. Children who miss these experiences are significantly deprived. Outdoors, children can have the freedom to explore different ways of 'being', feeling, behaving and interacting; they have space – physical (up as well as sideways), mental and emotional; they have room and permission to be active, interactive, messy and noisy, and to work on a large scale; they may feel less controlled by adults.

The real contact with the elements, seasons and the natural world, the range of perspectives, sensations and environments – multi-dimensional and multi-sensory – and the daily change, uncertainty, surprise and excitement all contribute to the desire young children have to be outside. It cannot be the same indoors; a child cannot *be* the same indoors – outdoors is a vital, special and deeply engaging place for young children.

6 *Outdoors should be a dynamic, flexible and versatile place where children can choose, create, change and be in charge of their play environment.*
Outdoor provision can, and should, offer young children an endlessly versatile, changeable and responsive environment for all types of play where they can manipulate, create, control and modify. This offers a huge sense of freedom, which is not readily available indoors. It also underpins the development of creativity and the dispositions for learning. The space itself as well as resources, layout, planning and routines all need to be versatile, open-ended and flexible to maximise their value to the child.

7 *Young children must have a rich outdoor environment full of irresistible stimuli, contexts for play, exploration and talk, plenty of real experiences and contact with the natural world and with the community.*
Through outdoor play, young children can learn the skills of social interaction and friendship, care for living things and their environment, be curious and fascinated, experience awe, wonder and joy and become 'lost in the experience'. They can satisfy their deep urge to explore, experiment and understand and become aware of their community and locality, thus developing a sense of connection to the physical, natural and human world.

A particular strength of outdoor provision is that it offers children many opportunities to experience the real world, have first-hand experiences, do real tasks and do what adults do, including being involved in the care of the outdoor space. Settings should make the most of this aspect, with connected play opportunities.

An aesthetic awareness of and emotional link to the non-constructed or controlled, multi-sensory and multi-dimensional natural world is a crucial component of human well-being, and increasingly absent in young children's lives. The richness of cultural diversity is an important part of our everyday world; this can and should be explored by children through outdoor experiences. Giving children a sense of belonging to something bigger than the immediate family or setting lays foundations for living as a community.

8 *Young children should have long periods of time outside. They need to know that they can be outside every day, when they want to and that they can develop their ideas for play over time.*
High-quality play outdoors, where children are deeply involved, only emerges when they know they are not hurried. They need to have time to develop their use of spaces and resources and uninterrupted time to develop their play ideas, or

to construct a place and then play in it or to get into problem-solving on a big scale. They need to be able to return to projects again and again until 'finished' with them.

Slow learning is good learning, giving time for assimilation. When children can move between indoors and outside, their play or explorations develop further still. Young children also need time (and places) to daydream, look on or simply relax outside.

9 *Young children need challenge and risk within a framework of security and safety. The outdoor environment lends itself to offering challenge, helping children learn how to be safe and to be aware of others.*
Children are seriously disadvantaged if they do not learn how to approach and manage physical and emotional risk. They can become either timid or reckless, or be unable to cope with consequences. Young children need to be able to set and meet their own challenges, become aware of their limits and push their abilities (at their own pace), be prepared to make mistakes and experience the pleasure of feeling capable and competent. Challenge and its associated risks are vital for this. Young children also need to learn how to recognise and manage risk as life skills, so as to become able to act safely, for themselves and others.

Safety of young children outdoors is paramount and a culture of 'risk assessment to enable' that permeates every aspect of outdoor provision is vital for all settings. Young children also need to feel secure, nurtured and valued outdoors. This includes clear behavioural boundaries (using rules to enable freedom), nurturing places and times outside and respect for how individual children prefer to play and learn.

10 *Outdoor provision must support inclusion and meet the needs of individuals, offering a diverse range of play-based experiences. Young children should participate in decisions and actions affecting their outdoor play.*
Provision for learning outdoors is responsive to the needs of very active learners, those who need sensory or language stimulation and those who need space away from others – it makes provision more inclusive and is a vital learning environment. When children's learning styles are valued, their self-image benefits. Boys, who tend to use active learning modes more than girls and until they are older, are particularly disadvantaged by limited outdoor play.

All children need full access to provision outdoors and it is important to know and meet the needs and interests of each child as an individual. Young children react differently to the spaces and experiences available or created so awareness and flexibility are key to the adult role. Observation and assessment (formative and summative), and intervention for particular support, must be carried out outside. While it is important to ensure the safety of all children, it is equally important to ensure all are sufficiently challenged.

Young children should take an active part in decisions and actions for outdoor provision, big and small. Their perspectives and views are critical and must be sought, and they can take an active role in setting up, clearing away and caring for the outdoor space.

The Shared Vision and Values for Outdoor Provision in the Early Years (Vision and Values Partnership, 2004) is available as a copyright-free PDF download from http://outdoormatters.co.uk/wp-content/uploads/2011/03/eyfs_res_vision_outdoor_play1.pdf.

Further resources and support for being, playing and learning outdoors

Asphalt to Ecosystems: Design ideas for schoolyard transformation Sharon Gamson Danks (New Village Press 2010) – a very extensive, detailed and comprehensive coverage with many coloured photographs (North American focus)

Creating a Space to Grow: Developing your enabling environment outdoors Gail Ryder Richardson (David Fulton 2013) – The process of developing outdoor provision with an emphasis on children's participation at all stages, using real examples and colour images from settings involved in the Kent Space to Grow project (Kent, England)

Dirty Teaching: A beginner's guide to learning outdoors Juliet Robertson (Independent Thinking 2013) – directed at teachers in primary schools and parents: 'one of the keys to a happy and creative classroom is getting out of it' (Scottish focus)

Early Years Outdoors, Learning through Landscape's support service for all settings with children from birth to five years, www.ltl.org.uk or tel. 01962 845811 – superb, on-going web-based support for all aspects of outdoor play and learning

Effective Practice in Outdoor Learning Terry Gould (Featherstone Education 2012) – accessible and useful coverage of several aspects of developing outdoor provision with colour photographs, including the EYFS welfare requirements and involving parents

Environments for Outdoor Play: A practical guide to making space for children Theresa Casey (Sage Publications 2007) – focuses on the design process for very playful and creative spaces (the author is the president of the International Play Association)

Exercising Muscles and Minds: Outdoor play and the early years curriculum Marjorie Ouvry (National Children's Bureau 2003) – a core text that speaks directly to practitioners with much insight

Exploring Outdoor Play in the Early Years Trisha Maynard and Jane Waters (editors) (Open University Press 2014) – a more academic, critical analysis of a range of important issues around playing and learning outdoors in the UK and overseas

Inclusive Play: Practical strategies for children aged birth to 8 Theresa Casey (2nd edition, Sage Publishing 2010) – a thorough and deeply knowledgeable coverage of what inclusive play environments really need to be like (the author is president of the International Play Association)

Last Child in the Wood: Saving our children from nature-deficit disorder Richard Louv (Atlantic Books 2010) (North American) – a key book that initiated current movements in the USA and elsewhere to enhance children's connection to nature

Learning Outdoors: Improving the quality of young children's play outdoors Helen Bilton (editor) (David Fulton 2005) – documents the developments made in the Brent Outdoor Play Project (London, England), with lots of colour images

Making the Most of Outdoor Learning Linda Thornton and Pat Brunton (Featherstone

Education 2013) – very accessible and visual examples of outdoor experiences both within the garden and beyond, organised under the (revised 2012) Early Years Foundation Stage Framework

Nature and Young Children: Encouraging creative play and learning in natural environments Ruth Wilson (2nd edition, Routledge 2012) – focuses on fostering child development and a connection to nature in natural early childhood settings (North American)

Nurture through Nature: Working with children under three in outdoor environments Claire Warden (2nd edition, Mindstretchers 2012) – illustrated with many colour images of babies, toddlers and two-year-olds, this book is highly valuable for thinking about the natural elements needed in outdoor provision for all children, whatever their age

Outdoor Learning in the Early Years: Management and innovation Helen Bilton (3rd edition, Routledge 2010) – continues to be a core text that covers the deeper thinking about outdoor play, learning and provision

Outdoor Learning: Past and present Rosaleen Joyce (Open University Press 2012) – valuable insight into the history and legacy of key pioneers of current thinking about outdoor play

Outdoor Play: Carrying on in Key Stage 1 Ros Bayley, Lynn Broadbent and Sally Featherstone (Featherstone Education 2011) – helpful for teachers of 6–7-year-olds in England to see how outdoor play supports the National Curriculum

Outdoor Provision in the Early Years Jan White (editor) (Sage Publications 2011) – explores and examines the values that underpin highly effective outdoor provision and practice (the Shared Vision and Values as outlined in this book)

Playing Outdoors in the Early Years Ros Garrick (2nd edition, Continuum 2009) – written for students of early childhood education, its strength is how it poses real issues and works through the thinking required to deal with them

Playing Outdoors: Spaces and places, risk and challenge (debating play) Helen Tovey (Open University Press 2007) – excellent for research and thinking about both outdoor environments and the risk/challenge debate

Playing Outside: Activities, ideas and inspiration for the early years Helen Bilton (David Fulton 2004) – highly visual with lots of colour images and a strong focus on the adult's role before, during and after outdoor play

Potential of a Puddle: Creating vision and values for outdoor learning Claire Warden (2nd edition, Mindstretchers 2012) – explores the issues that surround quality outdoor play and learning to help settings create policy and practice that follows the Shared Vision and Values (as outlined in this book) (Scottish focus)

Risk and Adventure in Early Years Outdoor Play: Learning from forest schools Sara Knight (Sage Publications 2011) – an extensive exploration of the need for challenging experiences and how to provide them in an appropriate way

Spaces to Play: More listening to young children using the Mosaic approach Alison Clark and Peter Moss (National Children's Bureau 2008) – finding ways to learn from young children how their own outdoor environment can best be enhanced and developed for them

The Reception Year in Action: A month-by-month guide to success in the classroom Anna Ephgrave (2nd edition, Routledge 2012) – shows how planning for linked experiences across indoors and outdoors can operate very effectively for 4–5-year-olds in school

The Sense of Wonder Rachel Carson, photographs by Nick Kelsh (HarperCollins Publishers 1998) – the most beautiful and important book about the relationship between child and adult in sharing nature together

Too Safe for Their Own Good? Helping children learn about risk and lifeskills Jennie Lindon (2nd edition, National Children's Bureau 2011) – core and accessible text for thinking about risk and safety in early childhood practice

Under the Sky: Playing, working and enjoying adventures in the open air Sally Schweitzer (Rudolf Steiner Press 2009) – extensive description of the Steiner philosophy and approach to being outdoors

Young Children and the Environment: Early education for sustainability Julie M. Davis (editor) (Cambridge University Press 2010) – an in-depth exploration of what education for sustainability means for young children and early childhood pedagogy (Australian)

Your Brain on Nature: The science of nature's influence on your health, happiness and vitality Eva M. Selhub and Alan C. Logan (John Wiley & Sons 2012) – extensive and valuable survey of the research connecting health and learning to being outdoors and in nature

Chapter 1

Providing for play with water outdoors

What this chapter is about

- Why take water play outdoors?
- Providing water outdoors
- Clothing for water play
- Selecting resources for water play
- Storing water play resources
- Playing with water in containers
- Playing with moving water
- Mixing water with other materials
- Playing with the rain
- Children's books, rhymes and songs
- Further information and resources

> *Water is at the root of all life; without it we cannot survive and as such it connects to us in a root way. Outdoor play should allow children to be surrounded by water based experiences from jumping in a puddle to hearing it trickle over stones.*
>
> (Claire Warden, *Nurture Through Nature*, 2007, p. 41)

Why take water play outdoors?

Water is a magical, intriguing and soothing substance to which young children are strongly drawn and it has always been considered to be an important ingredient of early years provision as a powerful medium for well-being and learning. However, provision indoors usually has to be contained within a water tray and we need to manage activity in order to control splashes and spillage. While there are many good resources for exploring and playing with the water in a tray, children can have contact with it only through their eyes and hands, which limits the sensory information being sent to their developing brain. Practitioners will also have noticed how much children enjoy the feel and look of water coming out of a tap, such as when washing their hands. Running water has even more to offer for play and learning, but this is often quite a challenge to provide for children in an indoor environment, and often results in adults having to constrain and restrain children from doing what they really want to do with the water (hence our difficulties with children's enthusiasm for 'flooding the bathroom'!).

Offering water outdoors hugely extends the way in which children can interact with and experience it. The greater space offers plenty of freedom for movement and large-scale investigations, and flowing water is easy to provide outdoors. Children can move water from one place to another or see how it can make objects move, and there need be no concern for spills and mess. They can explore how water changes surfaces and substances, being wonderfully inventive and imaginative with their ideas and theories. With suitable clothing, children can play with water throughout the year, interacting with it using their whole body and all their senses. Water is very much part of our everyday lives, and through the weather it affects how each day feels: investigating and exploring water during or after rain is even more multi-sensory and further supports young children in their quest to make sense of the world around them.

Providing water outdoors

General resources for water play

Large closed container for transporting water, perhaps with a wheeled trolley
Outdoor tap with stop-cock or removable handle
Hose on reel with connectors for tap
Additional hose plus connector attachments
Water butt with secure lid
Rain clothes and wellington boots for children and adults
Rack for hanging wet outdoor clothing up to drain and dry
Storage rack for organising wellingtons in an accessible manner
Small rubber gloves for children in colder weather
Water trays and large open containers for play

It is important to think about how the water play you offer outdoors builds on and complements the experiences children have indoors in your setting and at home. Sometimes, simply offering similar experiences with a large water container outdoors can be a good starting point, but do encourage the children to make use of this different environment. Children will quickly realise that they can start to fill containers and transport them around the outdoor space because spilling water does not matter in the way it does indoors. They will also realise that they can use the water to cover surfaces or mix with substances such as sand

and soil. It is very likely also that they will want to bring things to add them to the water in the tray or to 'wash' them.

In order to provide enough water for these activities, you will need a large closed container to carry the water from indoors – camping suppliers will have a range to choose from. A wheeled porter's trolley for moving crates and boxes helps to make transporting such containers easier and safer.

If children are to make the most of water play outdoors, however, settings really need to consider installing an outdoor water tap or running a hose pipe from an indoor tap to the outdoor area (indoor tap connectors can be found in hardware stores), so that plenty of water is easily available everyday, whenever it is wanted. An outdoor water tap is an important fixture to consider when designing new or refurbished provision as it will support several aspects of outdoor provision, especially growing plants. It is useful to include a stop-tap in the indoor piping so that the water supply cannot be turned on from outside out of hours. An alternative is to use a tap that is removable when not in use (however, these can be easily mislaid). Garden centres supply long hoses on reels which can either be fixed to a wall or used on a stand: those with wheels can easily be moved to where they are needed. If necessary, join two long hoses together with a fixing kit, also available at any garden centre, so that your hose can easily reach wherever you need it.

If it is not possible to install a tap or hose, a water butt with a secure lid makes a good alternative. This needs to be raised 30–50 cm above the ground so that children can fit containers under the tap to fill them. Because microbes will develop in this water if left to stand for more than a few days and as children are quite likely to drink it as they play, it is prudent to fill the butt with fresh tap water for a play session, emptying older water onto your growing plants. Most children are strongly drawn to experiencing the cause-and-effect operation of the tap to fill containers, and frequent use will build finger strength and dexterity as well as providing fascination for children interested by rotation and things that turn.

Do not forget the source of water that is often available for fun and finding out, provided by rain! With umbrellas and good rain clothes, there are many ways of exploring it directly, or investigating what is left behind after the rain has fallen.

Clothing for water play

In order to keep fully engaged in water play outdoors for any length of time, children need suitable clothing so that they stay comfortable. Since it is children's feet, legs and tummies that get wettest, a combination of wellingtons and dungarees is ideal for most of the year, adding a jacket on colder days. In hot weather, the best approach is to have some large towels to hand and to ensure children have a change of clothes in the setting. For water play that completely liberates children, try all-in-one rain-suits with hoods. These tend to be lightweight and easy to move in, while allowing children to spray each other or tip water onto their heads. They can also be packed away into a small crate or kit bag for easy storage.

An important part of enjoyable and extended water play is that children's hands do not get cold, but suitable small gloves can be hard to find. Many garden centres now stock rubberised children's gloves for gardening that will go a long way to keeping hands warm and functioning in colder weather. Remember also that feet in unlined wellingtons get very cold in the winter months, and warm socks are needed too.

It is quite important to give children the task of washing down muddy clothing and hanging them up to dry so that they are made ready for the next time. This is clearly valuable for developing children's sense of ownership of the outdoor provision, building a sense of responsibility, capability and independence, and providing meaningful learning experiences. Time, organisation, expectations and adult patience all need to be considered so that children gradually take on this role and can gain the most from it.

Selecting resources for water play

There are many resources that can enhance children's explorations of water outdoors. Keep reminding yourself about what is special about the outdoors that is not available or possible indoors (such as space, scale, movement, mess and stimuli from the real world), so that what you offer extends indoor water play provision, rather than duplicating it. As the seasons and the weather change over the year, water will feel different and activities are likely to be influenced, constantly adding new dimensions. Some resources need to be available outdoors all the time, as part of continuous provision, so that children can always have opportunities to:

- experience water in containers;
- investigate flowing water;
- mix water with other things;
- respond to the rain.

For each of these, the resources you provide can be gradually added to over time, so that children's explorations, thinking and understanding can constantly develop and grow.

Storing water play resources

Give some thought to the best way to store and present your water play resources so that children have good access to them as the need arises. Lengths of guttering and piping are effectively stored in a plastic dustbin (drainage holes in the base will be needed). A wheeled trolley with deep wire-mesh baskets will

Figure 1.1 Suitable clothing liberates children's play.

make resources visible while allowing them to drain and dry off. If you use plastic crates, drill some holes for drainage and leave lids off until the contents have dried, to avoid the growth of mould. Plastic laundry baskets also make suitable containers, but do not put too much in each one as the contents can easily become jumbled. Laminated photographs can be used to label containers so that resources stay well organised. If possible, store these resources close to where water play will usually take place. Children's visual perception is quite different to adults' and they are less able to distinguish individual items grouped together in a container. Therefore, it is better to keep storage containers shallow, with fewer items in each.

Regular washing of water play resources with an appropriate disinfectant solution, such as Milton, is recommended. More frequent washing can take place with warm soapy water and of course the children will take on this task with enthusiasm – this should indeed form part of planned and spontaneous outdoor water play. As children get older, it becomes important that they are given the responsibility of caring for their outdoor provision in this way, alongside other maintenance tasks outdoors. Young children really appreciate being able to help, and thrive on this kind of involvement – play and tasks become intertwined with patient, playful and supportive adult interaction.

Older children can also be given the task of organising the continuous provision storage of water play resources so that they are available for self-access. Each step in the process of sorting resources into useful groups, deciding which containers to use for particular types of resource, considering the drainage that will be needed, photographing a sample of each resource, producing and laminating visual and written labels, and deciding where to locate each container on the shelves holds superb potential for questioning, discussion, rationalising, negotiating and skill-building. In addition, if the children have made the decisions about where things should go, this will result in continuous provision that makes more sense to their younger minds and which should be easier to tidy away.

Playing with water in containers

Resources for water play in containers

A wide range of paint brushes, from fine art to masonry and wallpaper brushes
Large and small emulsion paint rollers (look for those with extending handles) and tray
Household cleaning utensils, such as washing up brushes, scrubbing brushes and toothbrushes
Spray bottles, sponges, cloths, drying 'leather'
Kitchen and/or camping utensils – cups, bowls, pots and pans, ladles, etc.
Buckets and a wide range of other containers, some with handles
Colander, sieves, tea strainer, flower pots
Wheelbarrow

Washing up bowls, baby bath and laundry baskets
Dolls, doll or baby clothes, washing line and a variety of pegs
Builder's tray or grow-bag tray
Paddling pool
Sturdy two-step ladder

The simplest way to offer water play outdoors is to provide children with brushes and a bucket of water. Despite its simplicity, this interaction with water is deeply absorbing for young children as it gives them opportunities to explore their world in detail and find out how things behave: many adults will remember doing this themselves, suggesting that this activity has significant emotional content for the child. We can give children permission to 'paint' anywhere and everything outdoors and can, over time, provide a wide range of utensils with which to work. Collect brushes of all dimensions, especially decorator's brushes from DIY stores: from very fine artist's brushes for filigree work to huge wallpaper brushes that need two hands. Offer rollers and emulsion paint trays, sponges and spray bottles. This activity is also greatly enhanced, especially for boys, by providing a sturdy, two-step ladder so that children can reach high up. An all-in-one waterproof 'decorator's suit' would add further to the role-play possibilities.

Children will paint all surfaces available, such as bricks and tarmac. Wood, tyres, chalkboard and slate surfaces are particularly fascinating since they change colour and texture as they are made wet and as they dry. Try adding more types of surface to your outdoor space with this in mind. Observe children closely to find out more about what interests them in this 'painting' activity: some will be applying their current schema or mark-making interests and you will see ways to develop their thinking further.

Provide a large water-filled container outdoors with big kitchen utensils or camping pots (you could try to obtain some old school kitchen utensils such as a ladle and colander) so that children can use all their knowledge from the water tray indoors and apply it in a larger, freer scale. Try having more than one large container or water tray some distance apart and supply lots of buckets and other containers, so that children can transport water between them: a wheelbarrow will help too. If you have an outdoor water supply then children can be challenged to fill these containers using a variety of methods, such as with jugs, buckets, watering cans, hoses, pipes or gutters: children who love to transport things will find this highly engaging and it will also save you a laborious task.

Washing dolls, baby clothes and bikes or other outdoor equipment are all very popular activities with young children: supply washing up bowls, a baby bath, laundry baskets, suds, sponges and cloths, a washing line and pegs. These explorations are full of opportunities for language development and can develop into role-play themes with embedded literacy activities, such as filling in a booking form and making tickets for a car wash. Boys have been found to be much more likely to engage in mark-making through these motivational contexts. Make a

Figure 1.2 Through interaction with water, young children explore their world in detail.

collection of relevant books to share with children and develop the play and learning according to the interests your children show (see *Exercising Muscles and Minds* by Marjorie Ouvry, 2003, p. 67, for a theme plan based on *Mrs Mopple's Washing Line* [Hewitt, 1994]).

Children love to put their feet in water, with and without shoes on. Builder's trays make wonderful puddles when rain is not available. Two boys at Darnall Community Nursery were observed by delighted practitioners to perform a spontaneous dance routine by alternately stomping in a water-filled builder's tray, one responding to the other. A paddling pool offers the opportunity to dip bare feet in this lovely, therapeutic substance at any time of the year, as well as making a good rock pool or imaginary ocean.

Playing with moving water

Resources for moving water play

Watering cans with a variety of sizes and spouts

Squirting and spraying bottles with a range of mechanisms and ends (purchased from household suppliers and garden centres), including pump-action vacuum sprayers

Squirting and spraying bottles from recycled containers with different mechanisms and ends, such as shampoo, talcum powder and sauce bottles (ensure any cleaning containers are well washed out)

Plenty of one- and two-litre pop bottles, funnels of different sizes

25–30 m hose and reel

Hose attachments, shower hose and head

Pond hose (2.5 cm) and other pieces of hose or tubing in varying diameter and length

Water pumps, suction pump with siphon hose (beer making or petrol siphon)

Lengths of guttering and down-pipes

Down-pipe hopper, gutter and pipe connectors

Trellis, crates, string, Velcro strips or plant ties

Shower curtains, big plastic sheet, tarpaulin or clear market stall cover (from *Muddy Faces*)

Plenty of small umbrellas, including transparent ones

Large (golf) umbrellas or water-resistant garden parasols

Long-handled brooms (both child- and adult-sized)

When water flows, it has additional and intriguing properties. It has a very sensory feel, it catches and reflects light, it moves in a variety of ways and it has the amazing ability to make other things move. Running water has a huge potential for raising questions, investigation, experimentation and problem-solving, especially for children fascinated by lines (trajectories), movement and enclosure. Exploring moving water in a playful way will help children to get to grips with some of the big questions about how the world works, including how substances behave in a world filled with gravity.

The first area of fascination is with watering cans – provide a range of sizes and spouts, including some with spray ends. Cans with fine open ends (for indoor houseplants) are likely to be used to mark-make on paving and tarmac as children realise they can control the water flow to make trails, patterns and emergent letter shapes. Children will also willingly take responsibility for keeping growing plants watered (make sure the plant containers have good drainage!).

Fast-moving water behaves quite differently to gently flowing water. Offering a selection of spraying and squirting bottles and devices will enable children to experiment with how water can be made to squirt and spray. Over time, a range of these with a variety of spray mechanisms can be collected to further develop skills and use. As well as the fascination with the water's behaviour and what it does as it hits objects and surfaces, this is an effective way to experience the very important connection between 'cause' and 'effect'. That two separate phenomena are connected through cause and effect helps children to construct ideas and theories about how the world works (theory-making) and once this happens they can also start to predict what *might* happen through imagining into the future. All of this experience is highly valuable for building the thinking skills for both scientific and creative thought. In addition to this, it feels amazing to be the one who is causing these things to happen and to see the effect of your own actions. Such experiences of influence and control are powerful at building self-image and self-esteem, so it is not surprising that children love to play endlessly in these ways! Try also making holes in large pop bottles and down-pipes so that children can explore leakage and the trajectories of the water as it comes out.

Hose pipes come with sets of attachments so that a variety of effects can be produced, from gentle sprinkler and spray to forceful jet; you can also try linking in a shower head. There is nothing quite like hose play on a hot day, but this can take place throughout the year with all-in-one rain-suits. The child handling the hose can gain from the feeling of being in control, which can be especially good for the more timid child, while others can enjoy the sensation of water covering or enclosing their body: clear boundaries need to be in place about who and where gets wet! Try draping a clear shower curtain or large piece of plastic sheeting over your climbing frame so that children can paint or spray on both sides with water or runny paint and watch the coloured drips make their way down the surface. With a hosepipe this can turn into an experience akin to being under a waterfall; try it with big umbrellas or parasols too. It might also lead on to experiments with making sounds and it is even possible to create a rain-storm 'symphony' by changing the water flow via an adjustable hose attachment.

Because of the space available, water can be moved on a grand scale outdoors. Cut household guttering and down-pipes (available from DIY centres) into shorter lengths of approximately one metre with a strong hacksaw and smooth the rough ends with coarse sandpaper. These become versatile resources with many uses other than water play and are easily stored outside. Because of their large size, children need to collaborate and work together in order to achieve their plans – so these experiences are very effective in encouraging communication and supporting personal and social development. Boys are particularly drawn to this kind of play, finding explorations and challenges to maintain interest over considerable periods of time (see *Playing in the Gutters* by Sue Dinwiddie). Provide resources such as milk crates to make ramps for the pipes, garden trellis so that a range of angles can be made and string, Velcro strips or plant ties so that guttering and pipes can be attached to fences. Extend the play over time by introducing additional resources, such as down-pipe hoppers and Y-connections, and new problems to solve, such as moving plastic ducks with the water flow, making dams or getting a water supply from the tap to the growing plants.

A great use of a length of wooden or mesh fencing is to create a 'water wall' by attaching a wide variety of containers and tubes to the upright surface, so that water can be made to cascade down in a sequence of motions. This can be done in many ways and with all sorts of resources, but is best set up so that children are encouraged to change the arrangement over time. If it is static, interest is likely to wane, whereas the wall will have much more educational value if it is interactive and can be developed by children and adults working together. There are many blog posts and Pinterest boards on the Internet that will feed ideas and enthusiasm for this useful idea (see resources at the end of the chapter).

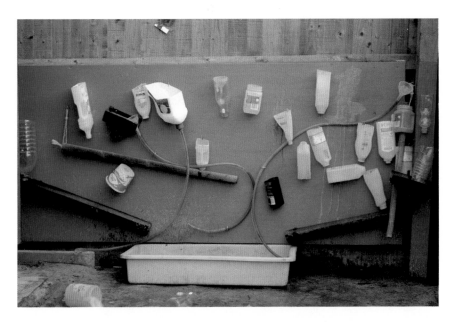

Figure 1.3 Flowing water can provide strong experiences of cause, effect and making things happen.

Children will also show a fascination for where the water drains to and where it goes from there, so theories can be developed as to why it runs down some slopes but not others, why it collects in some places but not others, and children might enjoy creating a group story about where the water has gone and what it is meeting under the ground. At this age, *all* ideas and theories are equally valid as we most want children to ask questions and theorise imaginatively – the more creative the better! Provide long-handled brooms as many children will enjoy sweeping collected water and helping it on its way.

There are many commercial water features which can be installed in early years gardens and these work particularly well as part of a quiet area designed for sensory and reflective activities. Remember that young children may drink the water so a mechanism to clean water that is recycled, such as ultrasound, will need to be considered.

Mixing water with other materials

Figure 1.4 Scientists at work exploring the magic of mixing.

Resources for mixing water with other materials

Sand
Soil
Baking and cooking equipment, kitchen utensils
Small containers and bottles (such as food colouring bottles) with lids
Special items such as pestle and mortar, meat baster, ice-cream server
Plasterer's tools for use with 'mortar'
Soap flakes, bubble mix, washing up liquid
Bubble wands, whisks, sieves

A special box of equipment for making pies, stews and perfumes

A range of baking trays and tins, small saucepans
Baskets for collecting plant material
Jugs, colander, large and small bowls
Kitchen utensils (several common and a few less usual): spoons, whisks, masher, ladle, ice-cream server

Turkey baster, pipettes, funnels
Sieves and strainers, measuring sets, pastry cutters
Small paint brush, egg brush, lolly sticks
Egg cups and very small bowls
Small bottles (food colouring bottles are ideal), sauce bottles
Pots of all shapes and sizes (recycled plastic food and bathroom product containers
    have lots of potential for play)
Small and large flower pots
Interesting and unusual containers, such as a sauce/gravy boat or a teapot
Pestle and mortar
Rolling pin and board
Wire cooling tray
Picnicware, tray
Treasure (for garnishing)
Magnifying glasses

It is important that children have the opportunity to mix water with other substances they find outdoors: both the process and the products of mixing water
and sand, soil, flowers or leaves are therapeutic and fascinating, and can support
imaginative play in some lovely ways. Many practitioners experience a warm
glow when they recall making mud pies, stews, potions and rose-petal perfume
and this is clearly a beneficial activity for young children up to and well beyond
seven years old. Two and three-year-old children are drawn to the basic activity
of transferring and mixing, but the act of causing a physical transformation soon
supports the emergence of imaginative thinking, where the mixture becomes a
cup of tea, coffee with sugar or a birthday cake. If mixing and 'concocting' is
provided as daily continuous provision, this will develop both in terms of its
complexity and in the skills involved over the pre-school years, building to such
actions as grinding, sieving and siphoning. Sand mixed with water also makes a
'mortar', which can be used to build with small bricks or to 're-point' the walls.
For four-year-olds, the 'what if' thinking of physically creating new combinations becomes richly intertwined with more elaborate imaginative play where
soups, stews, ice-creams, pasta, pizza and many other foods are produced. By the
time children are five, these concoctions often take on the shape of spells, potions
and more elaborate and magical substances, and for children over five complex
lotions and perfumes can be made, alongside the fascination of alchemy and the
full use of fantasy.

Practitioners need to identify and value the phenomenal learning involved in
such activity, convey this to parents so that they understand the many benefits of
this messy activity and organise provision so that it is manageable for all. The best
supporting resources can be collected from kitchen equipment such as mixing
bowls, baking equipment, a turkey baster, a pestle and mortar, small bottles, spatulas and wooden spoons. Whenever you introduce a new item, observe closely

Figure 1.5 Physically transforming materials leads easily into mentally transforming them too.

and work with the children to see how they make use of it and to teach them safe use. Keep these resources in a labelled container and ask children to use soil from the digging area rather than from plant beds, and to return mixtures to this area when they have finished, or use topsoil purchased from garden centres. Better still, work with the children to organise a dedicated 'mud kitchen' space so that this area of outdoor provision can be a major part of the overall outdoor experience on a daily basis – refer to *Making a Mud Kitchen* by Jan White for much more on this (see resources list at the end of the chapter) and see also Chapter 2.

A whole new area for fascination, investigation and fun is also opened up by adding bubble mix or washing-up liquid to water or using soap flakes (such as Lux) to make 'gloop': provide bubble wands, whisks and sieves.

Playing with the rain

Resources for rain play

Rain-wear, wellies
Large and small umbrellas (especially clear ones)
Powder poster paint, ready-mixed paint, paint sprayers, chalk
Plastic sheets, large clear plastic tarpaulin
Containers for collecting rainwater
Builder's tray, grow tray
Long-handled brooms, brushes, bikes
Tarpaulin, tents, gazebo
Big plastic containers, wooden and metal spoons
Waterproof camera, Dictaphone, tape measure

With a climate that so often results in rain, we need to have a very positive atti-tude to it! Children love the rain and will delight in any opportunity to play in it or with it. The key that unlocks this wonderful resource is for every child and adult to have suitable clothing, combined with enthusiasm from staff that matches the children's. Water play is a great way to make the most of a rainy day and all the previously mentioned ways to interact with water will be more multi-sensory and have more meaning for young children if they can carry them out while it is raining!

While rain is falling, encourage children to feel the drops on their hands, face and tongue. Given permission, many children will revel in the feeling of gutter overspill on their heads – for those who want to stay dry, supply umbrellas. Jumping in and over puddles is exhilarating, as is sweeping puddle water. Try putting poster paint into a puddle so that children can watch how the colour spreads naturally in intriguing formations, and then ride bikes through it to make marks on the tarmac (a squirt of washing up liquid in the paint will help it to dis-perse afterwards). Painting onto a large sheet of plastic while it is raining is great fun and produces fascinating effects as the rain makes the paint run. Give children chalk too to make marks on wet surfaces and in puddles (chalk does get used up quickly outdoors, so have plentiful supplies of cheap outdoor chalks).

Watch raindrops fall onto different surfaces, both vertical and horizontal, and see how the water collects, runs, disappears or stays: discuss ideas about why this is and where the rain has gone, being as imaginative as possible. The 'true' or 'correct' answer is quite unimportant here – using imagination, having ideas, constructing theories and feeling able to share them are all far more valuable and productive for building scientific thinking. Watch the patterns raindrops make when they fall into puddles; this is particularly effective in a builder's tray against the black background. Work out how the rain makes its way from roofs to drain via the guttering and down-pipes; and where it might go from there. Offer chil-dren a camera (a waterproof digital type) to record the images and patterns that interest them: compile a book with the results and add children's comments. Listen to, and perhaps record, the sound the rain makes on windows, roofs, leaves, the climbing frame and umbrellas and to the gurgles in guttering pipes. This can be enhanced by setting up a tarpaulin, tent or gazebo (or simply a parasol umbrella), so that a group can be cosily underneath together – have a special snack, tell a relevant story or make a rain dance by patting different parts of the body and stamping. Big plastic containers can become drums with wooden spoons as drumsticks so that children can respond to the sounds and feelings of the rain, either under the tarpaulin or out in the open.

Places around the world where rain is common tend to have a wonderfully extensive vocabulary to describe it and express their feelings about it. Think about all the words and phrases associated with water and with rain, and be ready to introduce this language playfully in the relevant context so that children can enjoy the use of language and play with bringing in their own ways of expressing personal experiences and feelings. Consider the quality of the rain itself – such as spitting, drizzle, mist, light, shower, heavy, pouring, storm, hurricane – and local phrases people use – such as 'bucketing down', 'throwing it down', 'raining cats and dogs', 'raining stair rods' and 'raining sideways' (in strong wind). There will be many more lovely words and phrases in languages other than English too. Gather words to describe what rain does to people and things – wet, wetter, wettest, soaked, drenched – and how water behaves as it falls and gathers during a rainfall – drip, drop, splish, splash, splosh, plip, plop, trickle, spill, overflow, gush,

Figure 1.6 Children naturally pay attention to this beautiful, fascinating and exciting phenomenon.

cascade. Finally, there are many words to describe the water that gathers as a result of rain – rivulet, puddle, ditch, flood, pond, river, lake, sea and ocean.

After rainfall, find out where the rain has collected and what it has done to things in the outdoor area. As the ground dries, use this water to make marks and patterns with brushes, brooms, feet and wheels. Children will love to help to wipe wet equipment dry, enjoying the responsibility and learning more about how materials behave in this fascinating world of ours. Some children might want to devise a way of collecting rainwater so that it goes onto the plants they are growing next time it rains. Help children understand that water is a limited and precious resource for the planet. Take every opportunity too to experience and investigate other forms of water that the weather brings us: dew, frost, ice and snow.

> *Through play ... he adds to his knowledge of the world ... No experimental scientist has a greater thirst for new facts than an ordinary healthy active child.*
>
> (Susan Isaacs, *The Nursery Years*, 1929)

Rhymes and songs

Ding Dong Bell, Pussy's in the Well
Dr Foster Went to Gloucester
Five Little Raindrops
Five Little Speckled Frogs
I Hear Thunder
I'm a Little Teapot
Incy Wincy Spider
It's Raining, It's Pouring
It's Raining Men
Jack and Jill Went up the Hill
Mud, Mud, Glorious Mud
Rain on the Green Grass
Rain, Rain, Go Away
Row, Row, Row Your Boat
Singing in the Rain
Somewhere over the Rainbow
The Rain in Spain
The Rainbow Song
The Day I Went to Sea
Umbrella, Ella, Ella

Children's books to support water play

A Walk by the River Sally Hewitt (Franklin Watts 2005)
Billy's Bucket Kes Gray and Garry Parsons (Red Fox 2003)
Brilliant Boats Tony Mitton and Ant Parker (Kingfisher 2002)
Coral Goes Swimming Simon Puttock and Stephen Lambert (Hodder Children's Books 2000)
Doing the Washing Sarah Garland (Francis Lincoln Children's Books 2009)

Mr Archimedes' Bath Pamela Allen (Puffin 1994)
Mr Gumpy's Outing John Burningham (Puffin 1978)
Mrs Lather's Laundry Allan Ahlberg and Andre Amstutz (Puffin Books 1981)
Mrs Mopple's Washing line Anita Hewitt (Red Fox 1994)
One World Michael Foreman (Anderson Press 1990)
Sixes and Sevens John Yeoman and Quentin Blake (Andersen Press 2011)
Squeaky Clean Simon Puttock and Mary McQuillan (Red Fox 2001)
The Journey Scott Mann and Neil Griffiths (Storysack Ltd 2001)
The Pig in the Pond Martin Waddell and Jill Barton (Walker Books 1992)
★*The Water Hole* Graeme Base (Puffin Books 2001)
★*The Wild Washerwomen* John Yeoman and Quentin Blake (Andersen Press 2009)
The World Around Us: What is an ocean? Monica Hughes (Harcourt Education 2005)
Threadbear Mick Inkpen (Hodder & Stoughton 1990)
Time to Get out of the Bath, Shirley John Burningham (Red Fox 1999)
Using Water (Exploring Earth's resources series) Sharon Katz Cooper (Raintree Publishers: Harcourt Education 2007)
Washing! (Small world series) Gwenyth Swain (Zero to Ten 2005)
Washing Line Jez Alborough (Walker Books 1993)
Water Cassie Mayer (Heinemann Library: Pearson Education 2008)
Water Frank Asch (Voyager Books 2000)
★*Water: Exploring the science of everyday materials* Nicola Edwards and Jane Harris (A&C Black 1999)
Wave Suzy Lee (Chronicle Books 2008)
Who Sank the Boat? Pamela Allen (Puffin 1988)

Children's books to support rain play

★*Alfie's Feet* Shirley Hughes (Red Fox 2004)
All Afloat on Noah's Boat! Tony Mitton and Guy Parker-Rees (Orchard Books 2006)
James and the Rain Karla Kuskin and Reg Cartwright (Simon & Schuster Books for Young Readers 1995)
Let's Look at a Puddle (Material Detectives: Water) (Raintree Publishers 2006)
Lila and the Secret of Rain David Conway and Jude Daly (Frances Lincoln Children's Books 2007)
Listen to the Rain Bill Martin Jr and John Archambault (Henry Holt & Company 1988)
Mrs Wishy-Washy and *Splishy Sploshy Day* Joy Cowley and Elizabeth Fuller (Shortland 2001)
Noah's Ark Lucy Collins (Walker Books 1993)
Ollie and Me: Out and about Shirley Hughes (Red Fox 2002)
One Rainy Day M. Christina Butler and Tina MacNaughton (Little Tiger Press 2008)
Puddles Jonathan London (Puffin Books 1997)
Red Rubber Boot Day Mary Lyn Ray and Lauren Stringer (Voyager Books 2005)
Splish, Splash, Splosh! A book about water Mick Manning and Brita Granstrom (Franklin Watts 2004)
Splosh! Mick Inkpen (Hodder Children's Books, Little Kippers 1998)
The Drop Goes Plop: A first look at the water cycle Sam Goodwin (Hodder Wayland 1998)
The Other Ark Lynley Dodd (Puffin Books 2006)
★*The Rain Door* Russell Hoban and Quentin Blake (Gollancz Children's Paperbacks 1995)

★*The Rainmaker* Barbara Todd (Annick Press 2003)

The Rainy Day Anna Milbourne and Sarah Gill (Usborne Publishing 2005)

The Thingamabob Il Sung Na (Meadowside Children's Books 2008)

Wet World Norma Simon (Walker Books 1995)

What Is Weather: Rain Miranda Ashwell and Andy Owen (Heinemann Library: Reed Educational & Professional Publishing 1999)

Who Likes Rain? Wong Herbert Yee (Henry Holt & Company 2007)

Children's books to support mixing and mud kitchen play

Delicious Helen Cooper (Doubleday 2006)

Fantastic Cocktails and Mixed Drinks Family Circle (Murdoch Books 1994)

Goldilocks and the Three Bears Nicola Baxter and Liz Pichon (Ladybird Books 1999)

Ice Cream Machine Book: Frozen delights from homemade ice creams and sorbets to sauces and desserts Rosemary Moon (Apple Press 2006)

Mama Panya's Pancake: A village tale from Kenya Mary and Rich Chamberlin and Julia Cairns (Barefoot Books 2006)

★*Memory Bottles* Beth Shosan and Katie Pamment (Meadowside Children's Books 2004)

Mud Mary Lyn Ray and Lauren Stringer (Voyager Books 1996)

Mudlarks in *Out and About* Shirley Hughes (Walker Books 2005)

Mud Pie Annie Sue Buchanan and Dana Shafer (Zonder Kids 2001)

Mud Pies and Other Recipes Marjorie Winslow (The New York Review of Books 1998 – originally 1961)

Mud Puddle Robert Munsch and Sami Suomalainen (Annick Press 2008)

Pancakes, Pancakes Eric Carle (Aladdin Paperbacks 1991)

Pie in the Sky Lois Ehlert (Harcourt Inc. 2004)

Princess Pigsty Cornelia Funke and Kerten Meyer (Chicken House 2007)

★*Professor Puffendorf's Secret Potions* Robin Tzannes and Korky Paul (Oxford University Press 1992)

Pumpkin Soup by Helen Cooper (Picture Corgi Books 1999)

Spells Emily Gravett (Macmillan Children's Books 2008)

Stone Soup Jess Stockham (Child's Play 2006)

The Australian Women's Weekly range of small, full-colour illustrated recipe books: Café Cakes; Cheesecakes, Pavlovas and Trifles; Jams & Jellies; Pickles & Chutneys; Casseroles; Curries; Outdoor Eating

The Essential Soup Cookbook The Australian Women's Weekly (ACP Magazines 2000)

The Mud Family Betsy James and Paul Morin (Oxford University Press 1994)

The Slimy Book Babette Cole (Red Fox 2003)

Further information and resources

Brush Daniel Rozensztroch and Shiri Slavin (Pointed Leaf Press 2005) – a remarkable photographic collection of hundreds of household brushes of all uses and designs

Early Excellence has a range of water play resources, www.earlyexcellence.com

Fascination of Water: Puddles – resource book for learning through rain and puddle play, with many colour photographs, by Claire Warden (Mindstretchers 2013)

Google Images has several stunning pages of images of water splashes, drops and other features of water and rain; try also *Flickr* and other image sites on the Internet

Learning through Landscapes can supply supporters and members with information about water play, water features and rain-wear suppliers, www.ltl.org.uk

Let the Children Play blog site has many posts about water play, water walls and mud kitchens – also links to other blog sites and Pinterest sites with fantastic ideas and images (www.letthechildrenplay.net)

Mindstretchers supplies high-quality rain-wear and other resources for 'walking, running and splashing', www.mindstretchers.co.uk

Muddy Faces is a great supplier of resources focused on playing with water outdoors, including a large, very robust clear tarpaulin and rain-wear; it also has a superb range of resources for mud kitchens, including special collections developed with Jan White, www.muddyfaces.co.uk

The *Cosy* catalogue includes many great resources to support and extend water play outdoors, www.cosydirect.com

Our World of Water Beatrice Hollyer and Oxfam – an excellent selection of stories of children's daily lives with water around the world (Frances Lincoln Children's Books 2008)

Oxfam teacher's site for information and resources looking at the role of water in people's lives around the world, www.oxfam.org.uk/education/resources/water-week-introductory-resources

Playing in the Gutters: Enhancing children's cognitive and social play Sue Dinwiddie, www.communityplaythings.com/c/resources/articles/index.htm (April 2005 newsletter: Sand and water play)

Playing with the Rain Jan White – an inspiring and visual guide to the beauty and value of rain as an exciting and wonderful resource for play, rather than a hindrance to being outdoors. Downloadable PDF from www.muddyfaces.co.uk (located under 'Water Play')

Making a Mud Kitchen Jan White – an exciting and comprehensive booklet on all aspects of supporting and developing mud pie play, with fabulous images and a list of further resources. Free downloadable PDF from www.muddyfaces.co.uk (located under 'Mud Kitchens')

Rainy Days in the Lake District – a photographer's view of rain and flood in the Lakes by Val Corbett (Frances Lincoln 2012)

Swell: A year of waves – full of colour images of waves in seas and oceans around the world by Evan Slater (Chronicle Books 2012)

The Mud Center: Recapturing childhood Becky Jensen and Julie Bullard, www.communityplaythings.com/resources/articles (February 2005 newsletter: Dramatic play)

Water Aid website with information and resources about the role of water in the lives of children around the world, www.wateraid.org. Water Aid has also produced *Water Splash*, a teaching pack for the early years with an accompanying set of eight colour posters, available at www.developmenteducation.ie/resources/climate-change-and-sustainable-development/water-splash-an-early-years-education-pack-about-water.html

Waves – a book of 30 colour postcards of waves in all forms by Rob Gilley (Chronicle Books 2008)

World Water Day is held annually on 22 March by the United Nations and other organisations, and *International Mud Day* is promoted by the World Forum Foundation on Early Care and Education on 29 June annually, www.worldforumfoundation.org

Summary

- Water is fascinating, therapeutic and full of potential for young children's learning and is therefore a major ingredient for every setting's continuous provision outdoors.
- Water is also one of the most important substances on the planet and for human life – it is therefore crucial that children have very extensive opportunities to interact with, explore and appreciate it fully.
- Water play can be endlessly and deeply interesting for young children, giving them strong experiences in all areas of learning and development.
- Suitable waterproof clothing and adult enthusiasm are key to successful and effective water play outdoors.
- Outdoor water play needs to make the most of the special nature of the outdoors, complementing and extending experiences children have indoors and at home.
- Water play outdoors can take a wide range of forms and can be offered throughout the year.
- Young children love rain: make the most of the rain itself and enhance water play by making it available on rainy days.
- Water play is vastly and deeply extended when children are supported to explore mixing water with other materials found in the outdoors, such as sand, soil and plant materials.
- Continuous provision outdoors is most effective when children can always have opportunities to experience water in containers, investigate flowing water, mix water with other things and respond to the rain.
- It is important to notice, value and share the wide range of learning taking place for individuals while they are engaged in outdoor water play: children will show us a great deal about their competencies, interests and development through this play.

Chapter 2

Providing natural materials outdoors

A child does not have to be motivated to learn; in fact, learning cannot be stopped. A child will focus on the world around him and long to understand it. He will want to know why things are the way they are. He won't have to be told how to be curious; he will just be curious. He has no desire to be ignorant; rather he wants to know everything.

(Valerie Fitzenreiter, *The Unprocessed Child*, 2003)

Natural materials and young children's play outdoors

As a child, I spent much of my play outdoors interacting with natural materials, especially with my siblings in our sand pit, which was simply a large hole in the ground filled with builder's sand. We had plans to dig to Australia, or at least to our neighbouring friend's garden; and our dog would enthusiastically help us. I used leaves and stones to make endless meals, and I painted all available surfaces with a sloppy mud mixture (slop-dosh). I produced rose-petal perfume to sell in tiny bottles, I made patterns with shells gathered on trips to the seaside, and I collected stone and pebble treasure that I thought was attractive or precious. I am convinced that this kind of play contributed to a lifelong love of the natural world and a strong interest in finding out everything about it. As a four-year-old, my daughter's summer was fully occupied with making innumerable 'concoctions' with substances from the kitchen, such as flour and sugar, and anything she could find in the garden: soil, gravel, leaves, berries, water. She spent long periods of time deeply absorbed in grinding, mixing and decanting. I looked on with delight and marvel at this deeply curious, inventive and imaginative child; and the scientist in her was clearly evident. Now, as a young adult she has a very enquiring, creative and resourceful approach to life. Again, I am sure that this play was significant in her development.

Natural materials are some of the best resources you can provide for outdoor play across all areas of learning and well-being. They are easily found; collected from the world around us or inexpensive to buy from many accessible sources. They are easy to store and present in appealing ways to children. Most importantly, they have excellent play value, stimulating and supporting a wide range of play and generating learning across the whole curriculum in a motivational and meaningful way. They are suitable for children at all ages and stages, with increasingly refined possibilities for play as children mature, from basic digging and filling to the complicated steps and tasks involved in making perfume.

We traditionally bring sand, water and other natural materials into the classroom because we know how rich they are as learning materials. However, they can only ever be explored and used in limited ways indoors because of the restraints we need to place on how children make use of them: mess and space limitations tend to contain and constrain play. How much better to take advantage of the freedom and stimulation of the outside environment, where children can:

- interact with the materials with their whole body, without the constraints of a tray;
- use all their senses with lots of movement and action;
- work on both large and tiny scales;
- transport materials to other places and use them in new ways;
- be relaxed about mess and so be more inventive and creative;
- make sense of the materials in their natural contexts;
- have more room to play alongside and with others;
- feel comfortable about the presence of adults beside them as they play;
- be stimulated by things happening in the environment and in the locality of the play area;
- experience materials differently each day, as the weather and seasons change.

The beach is by far the environment with most play value for children, so no wonder it is a favourite place to visit! Sand itself is a most magical, entrancing and therapeutic substance. The full menu of sand, water, shells, pebbles, plant material, open sky and weather creates endless possibilities for the combination and interaction of materials. Children can explore, discover, modify, experiment, build and imagine. Creating a beach-like sand area in your outdoor space will introduce a great deal of stimulus and support for well-being and learning in all areas, for all children.

Water adds substantially to the enjoyment and investigative levels of natural materials, and the combination of these two elements is unbeatable. Good risk assessment and daily risk management will open up a huge range of meaningful and satisfying experiences for your children outdoors. Establish codes of use with your children that enable all to benefit from these fabulous resources safely and effectively.

What do natural materials offer young children?

Natural materials have very high play value and contribute to all major areas of development. As resources for play, they are entirely open-ended and can be used in myriad different ways. They allow children to make sense of the world around them – first through direct contact with its elements and then as play materials for following their own interests and creative ideas. What other educational resource does so much, and for so little expense?

A good supply of natural materials can:

- Respond to the child's insatiable curiosity to explore the stuff of the world around them and their relationship to it. As children explore their world by playing with it, they are asking first, 'What is this and what does it do?' and also, 'What does this do to me and how does this make me feel?' Later on this develops into, 'What can I do with this and what can I do here?' and soon after, 'What can I make this do and what can I make it become?'
- Provide therapeutic play that is emotionally satisfying and supports mental health. Children often spend long periods of time lost in their own worlds as they handle, manipulate, explore and imagine. Natural materials can provide both the landscape for play and the resources for playing there.
- Promote awareness and emotional connection to the world around: playing with things that belong to the natural world; experiencing seasonal rhythms; enjoying the aesthetic qualities of natural things. This can lead to a desire to care for, and a lifelong interest in, the natural world.
- Encourage the development of sensory systems and sensory integration. Natural materials are multi-sensory, offering visual, textural, temperature, weight, smell and sound stimuli.
- Develop both fine-manipulative and gross-motor physical skills through, for example, digging or lifting and carrying heavy items, such as logs.

Figure 2.1 Exploring the stuff of the world.

- Promote the development of feeling, strength and dexterity in the hands – both in the skin through the sense of touch, and in the hand's muscles, joints and tendons through the internal 'proprioceptive' sense (see Chapter 4 for more on this).
- Foster imagination and creativity: their truly open-ended nature means they are very versatile and can be used and combined in endless ways and they are excellent for both solitary and shared imaginative play.
- Develop scientific and mathematical cognitive skills. For example, through observing detail, sorting, ordering and classifying, the basic skills of recognising similarities and differences develop. Construction and pattern-making experiences support mathematical thinking for number, size, measurement, shape and position.
- Develop symbolic cognitive skills. Using one thing to represent another underpins symbolic thinking and leads to being able to use our symbol systems of letters, words, numbers and musical notation.
- Encourage language through playful interaction, for example, using descriptive language for the properties of materials and hearing adults describe what is happening during exploration and play.

Natural materials are particularly effective at supporting children to explore their schematic interests (schema). A schema is a pattern of related actions that children repeat over and over, and through which they are working out how the world behaves. Individual children are often found to be quite driven to explore a particular theme and they will notice and be drawn to anything that fits into this idea, allowing them to investigate it further so that they can test and expand their ideas about how things happen in the world. Research and practice have shown that nearly all children get interested in some of these ideas at some stage; observing children with this knowledge in mind will show which theme or question they are currently working on. Schemas help us to make sense of the grand structure of the physical world and children work like scientists, building their own 'working theories' and understandings; so this work also builds up thinking and learning mechanisms. Therefore, an environment that gives children many opportunities to explore schema will be rich in thinking and learning. With plenty of natural materials and good supporting resources available, you are likely to see children burying, hiding and finding objects in sand (enclosure); filling buckets and wheelbarrows with gravel in order to move it around (containing and transporting); making lines, grids and patterns with twigs and shells (connecting, trajectories and grids); collecting, sorting and arranging items (placing and sequencing) and sending pebbles along a length of plastic pipe (going through). Schema-watching becomes fascinating as you come to understand how children are thinking, and these wonderfully versatile materials are full of potential for meeting children's needs for enthusiastically constructing and pursuing their own enquiries. Close observation also reveals how important such schematic interests are for firmly laying the foundations of many future concepts and approaches to learning.

The open-endedness of natural materials gives them another powerful role that is particularly significant in the early years of learning because they naturally lend themselves to being used *as if* they were other things in the child's world. The practice children have in imaginative play with natural materials of using one thing to *stand in for* (represent) another is very valuable work towards being able to use symbols. Symbols are marks or objects that stand in for something else, and we use many symbol systems in our day-to-day world – words, letters, numbers, money, maps, road signs and supermarket logos are just a few. This capacity seems to be built into us, but it only develops well through a great deal of experience and practice. If children are going to become good readers, writers and mathematicians, they need to begin with lots of pretending and representing throughout their early years. For this critical aspect of educational provision, rich and varied small-world and role play with open-ended, natural materials is the perfect and most appropriate mechanism for children up to seven.

Good natural materials for exploration and play, and where to get them

Sand and soil

Many *playground equipment* suppliers also supply high-quality play sand. *Aggregate companies* can supply large quantities of good quality sand: make sure that it is a high-quality grade and suitable for young children's play. Sand that is ground from sandstone can have fine particles that should not be inhaled. Triple-washed silver sand is recommended; the expense is worthwhile as the benefits of providing sand are so high. Sand that is supplied as an impact-attenuating fall surface is not as good for forming and moulding since it has rounded particles – good moulding 'sharp' sand has angular particles, so look for sand sold as play sand in preference. Ordinary builder's sand is coarse and contains high iron levels, so it is likely to leave an orange stain on skin (temporary) and clothing (less so) but this should not be harmful to children. For large sand areas, higher grade plasterer's sand does seem to make a good solution that is relatively inexpensive.

High-quality loam topsoil can be purchased in bags at any good garden centre and should be clean from animal pathogens. Larger quantities can be bought by the tonne or half-tonne from builders' merchants and this is less likely to be contaminated by dog and cat pathogens than soil from a garden. It is environmentally unsound to use peat-based compost as the bog habitats from which they are extracted are becoming seriously endangered. Peat-free compost is far less satisfying than loam as a manipulative material and does not mix well with water, but it does make a lovely and tactile material to handle in addition to good supplies of soil.

Wood: logs, tree trunk slices, sections of branches, sticks and twigs

Your *local council* and *wildlife trusts* have to manage trees or have materials that have been cleared from land they care for, such as branches and trunks. They may be happy to deliver wood from trees they are felling or pruning, so do not be afraid to ask! Alternatively, you might have cottage industries locally that make products from wood and who are willing to supply suitable materials, such as trunk slices and short lengths of branch. Check every piece for sharp points and splinters and teach children how to do the same. Cut off and sand down anything with an unacceptable level of risk – children quickly learn to keep an eye on their sticks and will happily smooth these off with coarse sandpaper. Planking and sections sold for decking also make excellent resources for construction play. *Treeblocks* supply several lovely collections of small natural wooden blocks in canvas bags (visit www.treeblocks.co.uk), *Muddy Faces* have an extensive range of wood pieces under the name 'noggins' (visit www.muddyfaces.co.uk) and *Cosy* stocks an excellent range of larger wood branch and trunk pieces (visit www.cosydirect.com).

Stone: cobbles, pebbles, slate, gravel

Garden centres and *DIY stores* with garden sections have increasing selections of aggregates, pebbles and interesting large stones for landscaping gardens. A bag of cobbles provides a satisfying quantity and it is possible to offer a good variety for little cost. *Builders' merchants* can supply gravel, pea gravel and other aggregates by the tonne or half-tonne. DIY stores also supply stone flooring that can make some very interesting surfaces for play with natural materials. *Home-making stores* often have small bags of polished pebbles and *pet shops* with aquarium sections supply a variety of interesting gravels and stones for aquaria (avoid artificially coloured stones, however). Young children are very aware of detail and will find much to explore even within a simple bucket of gravel. Play will be extended by offering a range of sizes, textures, shapes and colours. Children can paint a set of large cobbles with poster paint and coat them with yacht varnish to make further resources for play.

Plants: flowers, petals, herbs, leaves, grass

Flowers and petals make some of the most appealing materials for play. Children might use plant materials to make ephemeral patterns, for decorating constructions and as food for play in dens. Make the most of common weeds growing in your outdoor space or nearby: daisies, dandelions, buttercups; rose petals, cherry blossom; whatever is safe and available at the time. Make the most of what is in season so that you can offer really abundant supplies for exploration and play – dandelions are especially lovely and effective play resources while they are about in profusion. Some of the plants you select to grow will provide materials for play: scented leaves from herbs, grass heads from a meadow, twigs from woody shrubs; make sure you grow enough to generate a renewable supply and encourage your lawn and borders to grow 'weeds'! Mow grass less often to encourage dandelion and daisy flowering and when the grass is mowed, leave the cuttings for a day or two for children to play with it. Be alert to children who are sensitive to it, however.

Make sure children have plenty of opportunities to play with big piles of leaves. Visit parks for leaf-play sessions and bring back large quantities for further play and investigations (if dog mess is a problem, collect from the gardens of staff and families). Make colour photocopies of beautiful leaves so that the original colours are retained, then laminate some of the leaves so that they stay fresh for a while.

Seeds: conkers, acorns, sycamore seeds, pine cones

Take children out on collecting walks and encourage them to collect with their families so that you have plenty. Once again, abundance is something to aim for, so focus on what is seasonally and locally available. There is something special

Figure 2.2 A range of fascinating and multi-sensory materials.

about having copious quantities of a particular material that cannot be provided by having small supplies of several different resources. A large collection of conkers offers endless investigative play ideas with buckets, guttering and pulleys, for example. If you plant some of the acorns in individual pots after using them in play, you will have baby oak saplings in the spring (protect from hungry squirrels though!). *Hobby shops* and *home-making stores* often have small bags of shells, pebbles, glass nuggets and plant materials for flower arranging: check that these are safe for your children.

Shells, feathers, minerals

It is illegal to remove quantities of shells and pebbles from our beaches, but small collections can be built up over time if families help. Collect a range of types, colours and sizes, from huge to tiny. Aim to provide large quantities of small shells and a few large and special ones. Feathers take longer to collect but do form a nice addition – work on your collection over time and take particular care of these more delicate resources. You can soak the ends in Milton solution if cautious about hygiene. Organise shells, feathers and special stones so that they are presented attractively and accessibly, such as in tubs or the removable trays of a mobile trolley, and provide lots of small and interesting baskets for sorting them into.

There are several sources for small quantities of shells – for example, *Early Excellence* in Huddersfield supplies a lovely range of 'special' shells (www.early-excellence.com), the *Cosy* catalogue has a good range of interesting shells, such as giant barnacles (www.cosydirect.com), and *TTS* online shop has a nice bag of abalone pieces (www.tts-group.co.uk). *Mindstretchers* can supply some natural materials, including a set of rocks and minerals and a nice range of small baskets (www.mindstretchers.co.uk). However, for really satisfying play outdoors, large supplies of shells are necessary, and *Muddy Faces* is the best supplier for this, with a large range and mixed shells in quantities up to 3 kg (supplied in useful tubs with lids). They also have a good range of baskets for storage and transporting (www.muddyfaces.co.uk). Visit www.seashells.org and www.seashells.com for information about a huge range of shells, help with identification and lots of clear images (however, they do not ship outside mainland USA).

Providing natural materials outdoors

Providing sand

Sand is a wonderfully versatile material that is very responsive to individual children's interests, making it an especially important element of early years provision outdoors. Sand areas need to be as big as possible: the bigger they are, the more they will offer. Make them as deep as possible too, for real digging with lots of energy expenditure while making big holes and channels. Children can use their back, stomach and limb muscles, experience the sand with their whole bodies, dig deep and work on a big scale, work collaboratively and add liberal quantities of water. Consider having more than one sand area, as sand provides an excellent impact-absorbing surface and also interacts with other aspects of provision, further increasing the potential for play and exploration. As an example, consider how much sand can enhance play on a climbing frame if children are able to fill buckets to raise or lower with ropes in a simple pulley system.

Taking the indoor sand tray outside is a lot of effort for little gain. It is important to make the most of the differences the outdoors offers so that you extend and complement the range of indoor experiences, especially possibilities arising from scale, mess, movement, the opportunity to transport and changes in sand's behaviour caused by daily weather conditions. Try to make your sand provision like a beach, even if it is small. Use discussions with parents to focus on what your children like to *do* with sand in large play areas and on the beach, and build on this to make suitable provision that supports both well-being and development.

The edges of your sand area will affect how it is used. Edges that are flush with ground level will give easy access for children with limited mobility and allow children to fill and transport loaded wheelbarrows. Sand will spill into the surrounding area but children will be very willing to sweep it up, so provide plenty of brooms. They will also enjoy the process of sieving swept-up sand to clean it before putting it back to the sand area. Giving children such responsibility for caring for and maintaining their outdoor provision adds greatly to the learning potential. Raised sides hold in the sand, give somewhere to sit and are good for encouraging conversations while dangling bare feet in the sand, also providing good jumping-off points into the sand. They also provide adults with seating while observing or interacting with children's play. For this to happen, the tops must be comfortable to sit on for long periods. Bench-like seating along some of the sand area's edges also offers children the perfect work surface for mixing and 'cooking' with sand and water – be sure to provide some pots and spoons to support this important aspect of sand play. In a large sand area, seating and clambering can be provided with a tree trunk or large boulders, while a cable reel can provide a suitable work surface. Sand can also be sited in a grassed area with softer, slightly sloping edges where it will mingle with the grass, providing a new landscape for small-world play. Sand pits surrounded by grass are less prone to spreading as the grass cleans children's shoes as they move out of the sand.

With a water supply to the sand area, you can open up a whole new range of investigate possibilities and experiences. Very wet, sloppy sand behaves very differently to damp sand; it is fascinating how water first collects and then drains away; trenches in the sand can be filled to make moving water systems. Very runny sand feels amazing, and intriguing sculptures can be made by dripping the sand by hand. Use small sparkly items with very wet sand and shallow pans or sieves for children to try panning for gold!

Sand must be maintained in a condition fit for use. Covering large sand areas is not difficult, but the cover needs to be lightweight, so that it is easy to place and remove, and porous so that it allows rainwater to drain through. Solid covers reduce the air flow to the sand, making it stagnant, mouldy and attractive to unwanted mini-beasts. Garden centres and builders' yards supply a range of suitable plastic meshes and these can be weighted down with the small tyres provided for play: children will be willing helpers. Chelsea Open Air Nursery School in London uses a very successful fishing net over their large sand area that splits to accommodate a shipwreck. Consider making a custom-made mesh cover from greenhouse shading (a close nylon mesh fabric), tailored to the dimensions of your sand area, with heavy-duty chain sealed inside a hem turned around all the edges. This will lie securely over the sand and is very easy to place and remove. Animal 'chasers' that emit high-pitched ultrasound to deter dogs, cats and foxes from fouling the sand or soil at night can now be found in garden catalogues and from several specialist suppliers. Some settings with large beach-like sand areas rely on these as an alternative to covering their sand.

When creating the sand area, ensure that drainage of rainwater and water used in play will not be hindered: a layer of gravel under the sand should help, with a robust, permeable landscape membrane to reduce mixing (the advice of a landscape designer for your particular outdoor area can be helpful at this stage; see if any of your parents have this expertise). Encourage deep digging in play at all times to aid aeration and give the sand a deep and thorough flush and turn-over at least once a term. Diluted sterilising agents in the flushing water can also help to keep bacteria and algae at bay. The bits and bobs such as twigs and leaves that naturally collect in outdoor sand areas should not be seen as a problem; as on a real beach these materials can only add to the play value. However, a sand area sited under or near a tree canopy will benefit from a mesh cover out of hours – the leaves can then be collected as play materials themselves.

Shade needs to accommodate the movement of the sun, which is most harmful from midday to 2 p.m. in high summer. If shade-sails are used, make sure that they filter out harmful UV rays. Sand boxes with roofs often do not provide

Figure 2.3 Provide sand outdoors on as large a scale as possible.

shade where it is needed, so do select carefully. Your risk assessment for this aspect of provision should include knowledge of your own children, especially sensitive skin and hair, and the possibility of a child putting sand in their mouth.

Equipment and opportunities for outdoor sand provision need to complement and extend those offered indoors, rather than replicating them. To make this happen, plan for sand experiences across both indoors and outdoors at the same time, making the most of the differences in the two environments. Store twigs, shells, pebbles and other natural materials nearby to encourage their interaction with sand and soil.

It is important not to allow the sand or soil area to become cluttered with resources: cluttering hampers play, especially if the area is small. Every now and then try having no resources at all, so that children interact directly and simply with the elemental material. Sand, especially, is a beautiful, therapeutic substance that can be experienced more fully by sitting or lying in it, with hands and bare feet, feeling the cool and delicate sensations on the skin or trickling it through fingers and toes. Moist sand can be moulded into extensive landscapes with tunnels and roadways, with no need for any items additional to the child's imagination.

Providing soil

Earth really is a special substance that holds many fascinations for young investigators. Children can dig in it, turn it over, bury and re-find artefacts, make holes, fill buckets and wheelbarrows and then refill the holes. Although similar to sand, it looks and behaves differently and also holds the special fascination of creepy-crawlies; so it is worth making provision for both soil and sand if possible. When dry, it is hard and crumbly, but when moist it can be moulded with the hands; a good earthy loam also smells wonderful. Mixed with water, it is something else again. Sloppy mud itself intrigues as you make marks in it or paint with it, and feels amazing as it oozes between fingers or even toes! Mud with a good clay content can be moulded and shaped into bowls and all sorts of interesting sculptures, especially with the addition of plant material and stones (see *Nature's Playground*, pp. 52–54). But best of all, mud of all kinds makes excellent pies, cakes, soups, stews, ice-creams, potions and magic brews. Ensure cuts, especially deep ones, are covered with a plaster or gloves, to reduce any risk of infection. Compost is a poor substitute for texture and behaviour and does not mix well for mud pies, so do try to give children access to good-quality earthy topsoil.

There are two ways that soil can be provided to children, and each has its own delights and value. A mud-digging patch offers a very physical and whole-bodied interaction with soil on a large scale that children find irresistible. Such experience is important for foundational understandings around gardening and growing, as the medium in which plants develop, but is also full of developmental potential in all other areas of learning, especially personal, social and emotional development. Ideally, children need to be able to stand in the digging area so that they can dig with long-handled tools and use all their muscles: teach them how to use their feet on a spade for effective digging and an excellent physical workout. If you do not have enough ground available, try using a planter or large tyre (lined with 'weed control' landscape fabric to contain the earth) or make raised beds. Hygiene will be important: keep cats and other animals off with a weighted net, tarpaulin or plywood cover (and perhaps an ultrasonic or smell repellent) and ensure children get into the habit of washing hands carefully after play, especially before eating.

Mud kitchens provide something quite different to a soil digging patch, while also being much more easily managed. A mud kitchen includes elements of the much-loved domestic corner and cooking from indoor play, which are then hugely enriched through the special nature of being outside and the elemental materials children can work with there. Mud kitchens work well all year round and are best provided as a core component of continuous provision outside. Select a good location that gives access to a range of natural materials, including sand, soil, water and plants for foraging. Make an enclosed corner or other desig-nated space that includes walls for shelves and hanging utensils on. Ensure that there is room for several children to work together without hindrance. Working surfaces are crucial, at the right height and with enough space to work at with all the mess that creative kitchen work entails. Fit the kitchen out with a range of pots and kitchen utensils, and include a washing-up bowl for washing pots and hands afterwards. Mud kitchens do not need to be fancy and certainly do not

Figure 2.4 Mud kitchens provide a powerful mix of domestic play, baking and the outdoors.

need to cost much. There is nothing to beat the simplicity and character of creating your own unique kitchen from scrounged, donated and discovered items. And remember, the best mud kitchens are made in collaboration with the children who will be using them. For much more on this delightful area of outdoor provision, refer to the free resource *Making a Mud Kitchen* by Jan White from www.muddyfaces.co.uk and see Chapter 1 for resource lists. *Muddy Faces* also has an extensive range of resources, developed with Jan White, that stimulate and support specific aspects of children's mud kitchen play from two to seven years old.

Providing gravel

A large quantity of gravel has several play possibilities: as a loose material for filling, pouring and moving, as a landscape for small-world play and as a large number of small items for placing and arranging. Each piece of stone has unique details, which, because of their fascination with the miniscule, young children are observant enough to distinguish. Close up, the colours are very variable, as are shape and size, allowing for a great deal of sorting and pattern-making. Pea gravel offers a similar but different play material that is also pleasant to handle. Large play landscapes can be made with railway sleepers; if space allows, try having surfaces at different levels to add to the possibilities for use. Tractor tyres also make good containers (lined with landscape fabric or plastic sheeting with drainage holes). An array of different landscapes can be provided by grouping tyres filled with different aggregates, including sand – try also planting grasses or other robust plants and adding logs and large sculptural rocks. Be alert to the possibility of children putting gravel pieces in their mouths, as they may represent a choking hazard, although settings that provide gravel have not found this to be a problem.

Providing other natural materials

Large quantities of small items will rapidly become muddled and difficult to use unless attention is paid to keeping them well organised and appealingly presented. They will be used in a wider range of ways if they are stored in containers that can be taken to different parts of the outdoor area. Selection of a suitable container will depend on the size and weight of the resources, but do make sure that some can be moved by children themselves. Trolleys with deep and shallow removable trays and vegetable racks can be wheeled to sand, grass or paving – wherever they are needed. Plastic laundry baskets and bread crates make good containers for larger items, such as wood pieces, and can be carried by children working together. Some resources can be left outside in piles or in bins (ensure they have drainage) and a tarpaulin will prevent them becoming dirty from rainsplash. Baskets and clear plastic crates for lightweight resources can be stored on shelving in the outdoor shed. Baskets are a particularly appealing way of presenting smaller natural materials for sorting, classifying and pattern-making, perhaps on a picnic blanket; those with a handle are easier for children to use for transporting. Take close-up photographs and use laminated copies to label containers clearly. Images of children at play may also stimulate ideas for the next user. As previously discussed (Chapter 1, 'Storing water play resources'), the value of children making the labelling and organising the resources as continuous provision is well worth the time that it needs to be done effectively. Supplement large collections of readily available materials with some special items, such as bigger shells with mother of pearl covering. However, be aware that on tarmac and paving these are quite likely to get damaged, and it may be better to restrict their use to soft surfaces (such as grass, sand or bark) only. Plan so that there is plenty of time and support each day for children to sort resources back into their containers at the end of play. If materials have got muddled, have a big sort-out together, involving much mathematical discussion.

Figure 2.5 Sharing ideas with pebbles and stones.

Resources for use with natural materials

Equipment for supporting the use of natural materials needs to capitalise on what the outdoors has to offer that the indoors does not. The right clothing makes all the difference, especially when it is cold. Children need to be comfortable, but there is no reason not to use sand and soil all through the year. With suitable clothing, we can capitalise fully on the dynamic nature of the outdoors as the behaviour of sand and soil varies greatly across the year, and children can have the long periods they need for complex and satisfying play. The best resources for this area of provision outdoors allow active, exploratory, inventive and large-scale activity.

Resources for use with natural materials

Transporters such as wheelbarrows, carts and baskets on bikes

Buckets with handles for lifting and carrying

Bags, baskets, tool boxes, handbags, shopping bags: anything which can be filled and carried

Long-handled spades, forks, rakes (mostly child-sized with one or two adult-sized)

Child-sized trowels and other hand tools (metal ones are usually more effective than plastic)

Long-handled brooms and a dustpan and brush (sweeping is a very physical activity that children love and they can help to tidy up, returning spilled sand to the sand pit)

Old school kitchen equipment (such as big metal pots and ladles)

Bakeware and simple kitchen utensils

Mud kitchen resources (see Chapter 1)

Milk and bread crates

Plastic guttering and pipes

Garden sieves

Pulleys and ropes for transporting materials in containers

A water supply, hoses and watering cans

A range of magnifying pots and hand-held lenses

Camera for capturing children's work in progress and any products they want to record

Protective clothing, such as rain-gear. Dungarees provide ideal clothing when it is not raining as they cover tummy and legs while leaving arms free for movement

Child-sized gardening gloves (for those who cannot have or do not like direct contact)

Just as natural materials are good for supporting play in other areas of provision, many other resources go well with natural materials, especially those for imaginative play:

- small-world animals, such as dinosaurs, wild, farm and domestic animals and mini-beasts; have themed sets ready in easy-to-carry containers or the trays of a trolley;

- small-world vehicles, especially those that make tracks and with containers to fill;
- tiny versions of household items to stimulate house-making for tiny people and fairy tea parties;
- planks, small bricks and builders' tools for using sloppy sand 'mortar' and brick-laying;
- a large treasure chest or box, maps and artefacts to bury and find as archaeologists or pirates;
- something in the play house to represent a cooker and resources to create tables and chairs for a café or pretend snack time;
- resources for role-play themes, such as camping, pirates or an excavation/construction site;
- install hooks in nearby walls or use fences to make pulley systems with buckets and ropes;
- den-building resources: natural materials strongly support play in the dens and other constructions children have made.

Figure 2.6 Foraging and gathering is an ancient and natural drive.

Getting the most out of natural materials

- Remember your own childhood play and share memories as a team: mentioning rose petal perfume or fairy houses usually sets off good memories of playing with natural materials! Ensure all staff realise the importance of children's interactions with natural materials and give sufficient time to discuss and agree both your overall approach and the procedures for ensuring children's safety and well-being.

- Help parents remember and show them photographs, so that they too understand just what is going on through their child's creative play, and be clear about your policies regarding children's safe exposure to natural materials.

- Ensure the children stay comfortable and learn to keep their hands out of their mouth: establish the habit of hand-washing after play and, in particular, ensure hands are clean before eating food.

- Encourage children to use all their senses as appropriate. For example, by bringing children's attention to the smell of materials and the feel of flowers on their cheeks. Encourage barefoot experiences: children have very little opportunity to feel with their feet and yet we seek foot-massage therapies. Grass feels wonderful, as does sand and even mud for the adventurous.

- Encourage young children's awareness of and interest in the miniscule by sharing their fascination of small things and tiny detail. Introduce magnifiers when this seems appropriate so that children come to realise that it is possible to look even more closely, and then find images of natural materials close up to compare findings (see resource list for some useful sources).

- Observe children's use of natural materials and evaluate observations for possible lines of enquiry or development, so that planning builds on what children want to do and find out about. You will be amazed at the range of possibilities such observations reveal (see the example given in *Exercising Muscles and Minds* by Marjorie Ouvry, 2003, p. 34, on children's use of grass cuttings, where they threw it, gathered it, sensed it, imagined with it and used it to feed their gerbils).

- Having close contact with natural materials will promote awareness and interest in caring for the natural world, provided we also use appropriate opportunities to help children to become aware of the damage we can cause to nature and to treat their environment with respect.

- Collect high-quality images from the Internet, calendars and postcards and laminate them for use outdoors. Take photos of play and help children to photograph structures or patterns they make: use these to review and extend ideas with children, for display and for homemade books.

- Look out for instances where children use the open-ended materials to represent other things, as this kind of thinking is important for cognitive development. Use these records to plan with colleagues how to take this further in a way that retains the playfulness of the activity.

- Develop language to describe and appreciate the beauty, shape, attributes and properties of the materials. Make a book or display with colour images and the words you have come up with together, leaving space to add new words as they arise. Develop children's vocabulary of 'doing words' as you describe what they are doing: mix, grind, shake, sieve, dig, bury, find, uncover, reveal, sprinkle, pat, mould, squeeze, squash and so on.
- Help children retell and invent stories that incorporate their use of natural materials, such as making the Three Bears' 'porridge' or a story involving a spell mixture that gives special powers. Make the most of the potential for small-world imaginative play, using natural materials as both landscapes and play resources, such as houses, caves and tunnels (see fairy houses in Chapter 5).
- Encourage creative ideas for mark-making. For example, with a sloppy sand mix and paint brushes or with mud and sticks; make marks on loose surfaces with twigs or a rake; use wellies to make muddy footprints.
- Tell children that they are inventors, engineers, scientists, artists, mathematicians and story-tellers as they play, so that they see the high value you place on their own innate urge to make sense of their world.
- Emphasise curiosity, inventiveness, experimentation, discovery and fascination, and help children become comfortable about mess. Do not worry about mess yourselves: no creative workshop is tidy while it is in use!

Drink in the beauty and wonder at the meaning of what you see ... Those who contemplate the beauty of the earth find reserves of strength that will endure as long as life lasts.... The lasting pleasures of contact with the natural world are not reserved for scientists but are available to anyone who will place himself under the influence of earth, sea and sky and their amazing life.

(Rachel Carson, *The Sense of Wonder*, 1998)

Rhymes and songs

Five Big Ice Creams
Five Cream Buns in a Baker's Shop
Five Little Leaves so Bright and Gay
Little Miss Muffet
Mud, Mud, Glorious Mud
Pat-a-cake
Pease Porridge Hot, Pease Porridge Cold
Polly Put the Kettle on
We're Going on a Bear Hunt

Children's books to support play with sticks and leaves

A Leaf Named Bud Paula and Sara Shwartz (Rizzoli International Publications 1992)

A Stick is an Excellent Thing: Poems celebrating outdoor play Marilyn Singer and LeUyen Pham (Clarion Books 2012)

★*Find out About Wood* Henry Pluckrose (Franklin Watts 2002)

I'm Afraid Too Laura Hambleton (Milet Publishing Ltd 2001)

Leaf Man Lois Ehlert (Harcourt Children's Books 2005)

Leaves and Pods Josie Iselin and Mary Ellen Hannibal (Harry N. Abrams 2006)

Materials: Wood Cassie Mayer (Heinemann Library 2008)

Not a Stick Antoinette Portis (HarperCollins Publishers 2008)

One Leaf Fell Tony Speed and Minerva McIntyre (Stewart, Tabori and Chang 1993)

Red Leaf, Yellow Leaf Lois Ehlert (Harcourt Publisher's Group 1991)

Stanley's Stick John Hegley and Neal Layton (Hodder Children's Books 2011)

Stick Insect Karen Hartley, Chris Macro and Philip Taylor (Heinemann Library: Harcourt Education 2008)

Stick Man Julia Donaldson and Axel Scheffler (Alison Green Books 2008)

Sticks Eyelike Nature (PlayBac Publishing 2009)

★*The Giving Tree* Shel Silverstein (HarperCollins Publishers 1992)

Further information and resources – sticks and leaves

Bark: An intimate look at the world's trees – a truly stunning book of colour close-ups of bark on trees around the world by Cedric Pollet (Frances Lincoln 2010)

Beautiful Trees: Close-ups of amazing tree bark from around the world – a further collection from Cedric Pollett (Francis Lincoln 2013)

Bits of Wood/Bouts de Bois – colour images of land art created with pieces of wood by Will Menter (a wider resonance 2007)

Celebrating Dandelions for Earth Day – blog post on the wonderful value of dandelions for children's play by Jan White on 22 April 2012; visit: janwhitenaturalplay.wordpress.com

Everyone Loves a Stick – colour poster by Creative Star Learning Company, published by and available from *Cosy*, www.cosydirect.com

Extraordinary Leaves – close-up colour images of leaves organised by shape by Dennis Schrader and Stephen Green-Armytage (Firefly Books 2008)

Natural Architecture – a collection of colour photographs of land art by various artists working with sticks and other natural materials by Alessandro Rocca (Princeton Architectural Press 2007)

Nemis Lars Vilks – an enormous structure built from driftwood on a beach in Sweden; use images from www.atlasobscura.com and Google Images to inspire construction work by children

Stickwork – colour images of huge and fabulous installations created out of sticks by well-known land artist Patrick Dougherty (Princeton Architectural Press 2010)

The Stick Book: Loads of things you can make or do with a stick – fabulous compendium of ideas for making the most of sticks for children throughout the primary years by Jo Schofield and Fiona Danks (Frances Lincoln 2012)

Children's books to support play with stones and shells

Beach Stones Josie Iselin and Margaret W. Curruthers (Harry N. Abrams 2006)
Body Coverings: Shells Cassie Mayer (Heinemann Library 2007)
Carrying (Small world series) Gwenyth Swain (Zero to Ten 1999)
Everybody Needs a Rock Byrd Baylor and Peter Parnall (Prentice Hall & IBD 1974)
★*Find out About Rock and Stone* Henry Pluckrose (Watts Books 1994)
Heart Stones Josie Iselin (Harry N. Abrams 2008)
If You Find a Rock Peggy Christian and Barbara Hirsch Lember (Voyager Paperbacks 2008)
Let's Look at Pebbles (Material Detectives: Rock) (Raintree Publishers 2006)
On My Beach There Are Many Pebbles Leo Lionni (HarperCollins 1995)
Seashells Josie Iselin and Sandy Carlson (Harry N. Abrams)
Sharing a Shell Julia Donaldson and Lydia Monks (Macmillan Children's Books 2005)
Stones Eyelike Nature (Play Bac Publishing 2009)
Stone Soup Jess Stockham (Child's Play 2006)

Further information and resources – stones and shells

Pure Sea Glass: Discovering nature's vanishing gems Richard LaMotte, Sally LaMotte Crane and Celia Pearson – a seaglass collectors' tribute, with stunning colour images that will enthuse many children (Sea Glass Publishing 2004)
Sea glass calendars are usually available on the Internet (e.g. Amazon), which can be cut up and laminated to make a set of stimulating images or display to accompany beach pebble play
Seashells: Jewels from the ocean – a reference book about shells with good colour images by Budd Titlow (Motorbooks International 2007)

Children's books to support sand, digging and beach play

A Walk on the Beach (Nature Detectives) Jo Waters (Heinemann Library 2006)
★*At the Beach* Roland Harvey (Allen & Unwin 2007)
Beach: A book of treasure Josie Iselin (Chronicle Books 2010)
Billy's Bucket Kes Gray and Garry Parsons (Red Fox 2003)
Body Coverings: Feathers Cassie Mayer (Heinemann Library 2006)
Come Away from the Water, Shirley John Burningham (Red Fox 2000)
Dig, Drill, Dump, Fill Tana Hoban (Mulberry Books 1975)
Don't Mention Pirates Sarah McConnell (Hodder Children's Books 2007)
Flotsam David Wiesner (Clarion Books 2006)
George's Store on the Seashore Francine Bassede (Siphano Picture Books 1999)
Grandma's Beach Rosalind Beardshaw (Bloomsbury Publishing 2002)
Joe's Café Rose Impey (Orchard Picturebooks 1993)
Little Kippers: Sandcastle Mick Inkpen (Hodder Children's Books 1998)

Melrose and Croc beside the Sea Emma Chichester Clark (HarperCollins Children's Books 2007)

Mummy's Magical Handbag Paulette Bogan (Bloomsbury Children's Books 2005)

Scaredy Squirrel at the Beach Melanie Watt (Happy Cat Books 2008)

Seaside Holidays Monica Hughes (Raintree Publishers 2011)

Seaside Nature Paul Humphrey (Franklin Watts 2006)

Seaside Poems Jill Bennett and Nick Sharatt (Oxford University Press 2006)

The Feather Dot Cleeve and Kim Harley (Tamarind 2003)

The Magic Beach Alison Lester (Allen & Unwin 2004)

The Sandcastle M.P. Robertson (Frances Lincoln Children's Books 2009)

The Sand Horse Ann Turnbull and Michael Foreman (Andersen 2002)

Things to Do at the Seaside Paul Humphrey (Franklin Watts 2006)

Tip Tip Dig Dig Emma Garcia (Boxer Books 2008)

Further information and resources – sand, digging and beach play

A Grain of Sand: Nature's secret wonder – stunning colour microphotography reveals the beautiful detail of this ordinary substance (just use the images), by Dr Gary Greenberg (Motorbooks International 2008)

Playing in the Sand Naturally Ron King, www.communityplaythings.com/c/resources/articles/index.htm (April 2005 newsletter: Sand and water play)

The Little Book of Sand and Water Sally Featherstone (Featherstone Education 2002)

Further information and resources – general

Books by the artist Andy Goldsworthy, who works with natural materials in the landscape, are inspirational; try *Wood* (Harry N. Abrams Inc. 1996), *Stone* (Thames & Hudson 2011) and especially *Andy Goldsworthy: A collaboration with nature* (Harry N. Abrams Inc. 1998)

Calendars and postcards: there are many high-quality images available in card and book shops, such as the *Nouvelles Images* and *Editions du Desastre* ranges

Exercising Muscles and Minds: Outdoor play and the early years curriculum Marjorie Ouvry (National Children's Bureau 2003)

Fairy Houses Everywhere Barry and Tracy Kane (Lightbeams Publishing 2001); also visit www.fairyhouses.com (see Chapter 6 for more on fairies and fairy houses)

Fascination of Fire: Charcoal Claire Warden (Mindstretchers 2012)

Feathers – fascinating booklet documenting children's interests and play at the Woodland Preschool project from Sightlines Initiative, www.sightlines-initiative.com (under 'Online Store/Sightlines Initiative')

Following Children's Interests: Resourcing and supporting schemas through outdoor provision Jan White, Early Years Outdoors (September 2005), from Learning through Landscapes, www.ltl.org.uk

Making a Mud Kitchen Jan White – an exciting and comprehensive booklet on all aspects of supporting and developing mud pie play, with fabulous images and a list of further resources. Free downloadable PDF from www.muddyfaces.co.uk (located under 'Mud Kitchens')

Making the Most of Reclaimed and Natural Materials Linda Thornton and Pat Brunton (Featherstone Education 2009)

Natural Materials – a delightful booklet of creative explorations with natural materials by children participating in The Garden Room Art Project (part of a set of six) by Liz Buckler (email: info@mylittlebooks.co.uk)

Natural: Simple land art through the seasons – a really inspirational and visual book filled with colour images (with very little text) of work by nature artist Marc Poyet; many are similar to what young children might do (Francis Lincoln 2009)

Nature's Playground Fiona Danks and Jo Schofield (Frances Lincoln 2006)

Play Using Natural Materials Alison Howe (David Fulton 2005)

Surfaces and Textures: A visual sourcebook – a terrific way of sharing young children's attention to the minuscule by looking at the detailed beauty in everyday natural materials by visual artist Polly O'Neil (A&C Black Publishers 2008)

The Art of the Sandpit – Playnotes from Learning through Landscapes membership services, www.ltl.org.uk

The Mud Center: Recapturing childhood Becky Jensen and Julie Bullard, www.community-playthings.com/resources/articles (February 2005 newsletter: Dramatic play)

The Pest Control Shop has a range of repellents for sand and soil areas, www.pestcontrolshop.co.uk

The Sense of Wonder Rachel Carson and Nick Kelsh (HarperCollins 1998)

Why Dirt Is Good Mary Ruebush (Kaplan Publishing 2009) – a very accessible explanation of how beneficial germs support the development of a healthy immune system

Summary

- Sand, soil, stone, shells and plant material form some of the most versatile, multi-sensory and effective materials you can provide for young children. Owing to their variety, properties and open-ended nature, they offer very high play value.

- Outdoors, children can explore natural materials in their real-life context, in fuller and more meaningful contact and in more creative ways.

- Natural materials have enormous potential to enrich children's physical, emotional, social, imaginative and language development.

- Understanding the value of natural materials for young children is vital and needs also to be conveyed to parents through making their child's learning visible.

- Staff should agree their attitudes, overall approach and specific procedures for safe use. Careful and on-going risk management should aim to open up the stunning potential of these materials while keeping children safe.

- Sourcing and collecting natural materials is not difficult; they are relatively cheap and often free. Asking for donations from families is a great way to involve them in the life of the setting. Many natural materials can be stored outside, needing only a tarpaulin to cover and keep them clean for use.

- Utilise natural materials both as landscapes and as materials for play, exploration and investigation. Provide natural resources in several places so that they interact with other aspects of outdoor provision.

- Do not worry about mess: it is part of the creative process and should not be a problem outdoors. Children need clothing that keeps them comfortable while liberating them to get messy.
- Sand is a vital part of early years provision. Sand provision outdoors should significantly extend indoor provision and be as big and deep as possible. Make provision for children to transport sand and to mix it with water and other materials.
- Soil is a beautiful, fascinating and important substance that enriches children's experiences, so try to make digging available along with gardening. When children can mix soil and water to make mud, a whole new range of possibilities opens up.
- Creating a mud kitchen is a simple yet profound way to harness children's motivations and stimulate deep and meaningful learning. As continuous provision, this kind of play develops constantly on a daily basis across all of the early years.
- The resources that are most effective for supporting play with natural materials are household items and those that also support other elements of provision outside.

Chapter 3

Providing experiences of the living world outdoors

What this chapter is about

- Why are experiences of the living world so important?
- What does growing offer young children?
- Making provision for growing and natural experiences:

  - Choosing containers and where to site them
  - Choosing what to grow: what do you want your plants to do?

- Equipment and resources for growing and investigating wildlife
- Looking after your plants
- Getting the most out of growing and the living world with young children
- Children's books, rhymes and songs
- Further information and resources

> *Children have a natural affinity towards nature. Dirt, water, plants, and small animals attract and hold children's attention for hours, days, even a lifetime.*
>
> (Robin Moore and Herbert Wong, *Natural Learning*, 1997)

Why are experiences of the living world so important?

Something that is very noticeable about young children is their strong affinity with things from the living world – plants as well as animals. Too many children have little contact with nature in their daily lives, especially where families do not have gardens, or the adults around the child do not recognise or value what it can do for him or her. So a key element of the experience we provide for children in early years settings has to be close, personal contact with the natural world; and this is where your outdoor space can really come into its own. What young children need is 'everyday nature'. That is, plenty of time every day having real and direct, small-scale experiences of the living world around them.

Young children need a multi-sensory environment and plants speak to all the senses, so it is not surprising that plants are such an effective way to improve the environment for learning and play. Growing, especially vegetables and fruit, is a remarkably powerful theme for young children, with a strong emotional element, masses of learning in every aspect of the curriculum, lots of moving and doing and the potential for laying down interests and healthy habits for life. Digging, planting, nurturing, enjoying and eating reaches every part of the child's health and well-being. The living world changes from day to day as the year turns, giving endless new experiences within the predictable rhythms of the seasons and the cycles of life.

When you look closely, the everyday living world is intriguing and magical, and full of awe and wonder: think of the excitement when a child finds their first ladybird. Young children feel this strongly and we will have done our job if we can help them to retain this through their lives. Just as warm human relationships help to build an emotionally strong core, a connection with nature provides a sense of belonging that contributes to this resilience and offers emotional strategies for coping with stressful times. This will be very helpful for the fast-paced, ever-changing and materialistic lives our children are facing.

Children need outdoor spaces to have soft and enclosed elements in them so that they are nurturing, but for very many settings this is not currently the case. Where outdoor areas are open and hard, high-energy, boisterous play is likely to predominate; the needs of many children will not be met and some may not

Figure 3.1 Slowing down and looking closely yields wonder and deepens attachment to nature.

enjoy the outdoor play on offer. It is very important to also provide places for calm, peacefulness, daydreaming and enjoyment of nature, and plants are great for creating such attractive and sheltered quiet places. It is best to have plants growing all around the outdoor area, not confined to one separate horticultural or wildlife area, as children benefit from having these elements as integral to the whole space. Plants can contribute greatly to the overall feel and atmosphere of the outdoor environment, as well as to the provision of stimulating, exciting, satisfying and nurturing experiences and opportunities. A major benefit of growing plants on any scale is the wildlife, both big and small, that will live in them. Plants and wildlife can stimulate and support play, and the spontaneous events associated with them add a great deal to the learning potential of the outdoor classroom. Use plants wherever you can: for shade, shelter, boundaries, seating places, play places and for looking, smelling, touching, moving amongst and eating. And wherever possible, use plants that children themselves are involved in growing.

Growing is a great way to link home and setting. Parents are often keen for their children to have these experiences and find easy ways to become involved in what their child is doing in the setting. Some children may bring a lot of knowledge from time spent with relatives who are keen on gardening: be sure to use their expertise (and that of the relatives). Do not worry about your own lack of knowledge; it is best to start with something small and manageable and to learn alongside the children. In this 'companionable learning', the genuine interest that comes from *not* already knowing will be valued by the children, and learning will be much more effective as you discover and make meaning together. As confidence grows from learning and success, so you can make bigger plans. Everything you try out gives the opportunity for discovery and learning: adopt the attitude that the only 'mistake' is one from which you do not learn! This is a healthy way for children to learn, it gives adults the role of facilitators and everyone learns more by finding out together.

Much of the 'added value' of bringing nature into your outdoor area will be highly spontaneous, so it is important to have an approach that can take advantage of these events as they arise. Adults who are observing attentively to capture such opportunities need a planning framework that allows plenty of flexibility, with room for lines of development to emerge. Resources that will support children's predictable interests need to be collected and added to the continuous provision or prepared as enhancements. Above all, children need lots and lots of time outside to have hands-on experiences, to discover and to play.

What does growing offer young children?

- Learning through doing and a wide range of real experiences
- Strong emotional contexts
- Intimate everyday contact with the natural world, giving a deep sense of belonging
- Opportunities for lots of physical activity
- Opportunities for lots of sensory development and sensory integration
- Ways of working in line with their own schematic interests (schemas)
- Stimuli for working together, talking and sharing discoveries
- Opportunities to be responsible for the well-being of living things
- Interest in tasting and eating healthy food
- A softer, attractive and pleasant outdoor environment for play
- Foundations for attitudes and interests that can last through life

Figure 3.2 Gardening and growing offer endless opportunities for real thinking and learning.

Making provision for growing and natural experiences

Choosing containers and where to site them

Plants can be grown in even the smallest and most limited outdoor space, and are particularly important if your outdoor space is uninspiring or full of tarmac! Small containers can range from hanging baskets, tractor and car tyres, grow-bags, wooden barrels and old ceramic sinks to dustbins, all manner of recycled containers, such as kitchen pots and metal kettles, wellington boots and ceramic or plastic piping (try asking at your local builders' yard for unwanted ends). Larger beds can be provided with child-height raised beds, small plastic greenhouses (from suppliers or build your own) and borders and patches all the way up to an allotment, on site or rented from the council. A useful arrangement for young children is to make a patchwork garden by laying eight paving stones in a chessboard arrangement, so that different plants can be grown in each space or individuals can tend a personal spot.

In choosing what container or bed to use and how to set it out for use, there are some important things to consider:

- Does the container hold enough soil for the size the plant will grow to?
- Is it deep enough to give the roots room to grow well?
- Is there enough drainage so that the soil will not be waterlogged?
- Are all parts of the plant safe for children? Note that children will quickly learn about thorns and stings; we are concerned about serious harm.
- Can children reach over the whole surface without squashing plants at the front?
- Can children with limited mobility reach all the plants to touch and tend?
- Can children walk through the bed without treading on plants or compacting the soil (provide stepping stones)?
- Is the container/bed in a good place for the plants (amounts of sun, shade and wind exposure)?
- Can the container be easily reached by children for watering and tending? Young children's arms are relatively short so raised beds need to be quite narrow.
- Is the container/bed in a good place for play (will it complement play or will it get in the way of/suffer from other activities such as bikes and balls)?

Choosing what to grow: what do you want your plants to do?

There is huge potential for well-being, play and learning from having plants growing in your outdoor space, and so many reasons to grow them. As a whole team, with children and parents too, first have a good think about which aspects

Figure 3.3 Plants soften the play environment and influence children's play.

of provision you would like to enhance with planting. Then decide which kinds of plants will help with this and where they would best be growing in order to achieve your aspirations. You may have lots of ideas but it is wise to start with something you feel able to manage and to gradually add more planting over time, as confidence and horticultural skills develop. Having made some overall decisions, you can then research and agree on particular plants and placements. Here are some ideas and thoughts to help:

- Planting, growing and eating fruit and vegetables offers abundant learning and pleasure. Consult the children so that what you grow is of interest to them and what they will want to eat. For example, peas are tastier than runner beans, although beans are fascinating to grow. Select those that will be ready for harvesting during term time if you close for summer (such as strawberries for June and beans for September). Eating the crop (and finding the seeds) is a good way to set new children's interest off!
- Herbs in a kitchen garden have many functions, including being great for children's pretend stews and potions.
- A border or area designated as a 'picking border' can support play with plants – use fast-growing plants with abundant flowering. Some settings offer

older children a 'nibbling garden' where children are encouraged (with appropriate supervision) to eat specific vegetables or fruit straight from the plant (nothing tastes better than just-picked produce!).

- Flowering plants offer visual enjoyment, smell, shape and texture and will generally enhance the look and atmosphere of your outdoor space. Parents waiting to collect children will enjoy seats placed amongst a flower garden.
- Plants are fantastic for attracting wildlife, from butterflies, insects and spiders to birds and small mammals. Some shrubs and small trees can provide birds with food through autumn and winter, roosting spots in winter and places for nesting in spring.
- A quick-growing special wildflower seed-mix will burst into a stunning summer display that also is a haven for mini-beasts. Choose an early flowering mix if children are not present in August.
- Dandelions, daisies, roses and other flowers that children can pick will be very popular and effective for all sorts of play, such as pattern-making and mixing into 'cocktails' and 'perfumes'.
- Many plants can be grown for children to play amongst so as to enhance their play. Bamboo and tall grasses, small conifers and shrubs, willow domes and tunnels all provide spaces that feel different and which are excellent stimuli for the imagination; runner beans climbing the shed walls might evoke play about Jack and the Beanstalk. Use these spaces too for reading relevant books and making up stories together.
- Climbers provide attractive cover for shade and shelter; a pagoda with climbing plants makes a lovely nurturing and private spot for sharing books or simply chatting. Some wooden seats come with planters on each side and an integral canopy structure, so that climbers can turn the seat into an inviting mini-grotto. Russian vine ('Mile-a-minute') will provide good coverage very quickly.
- Grouping car tyres piled two and three high, amongst which children can move, is very effective at creating a small planted area (especially on tarmac), with its own seating provided by the tyres themselves.
- Really effective small-world landscapes are easy to create by growing grass or other small and robust plants in a tyre or even a builder's tray. Tyres have the advantage of providing a warm surface for sitting or leaning on during play.
- Plants can be used to make enclosed spaces or to delineate areas, so breaking up an exposed outdoor space. Grow such living boundaries that can be crossed in several places so that separated areas still interact with each other in terms of play.
- Shrubs provide all-year-round softness and cover for wildlife. Perennial plants offer the interest of returning every year, while annuals allow new children to make their own planting and feel a sense of it being their own space.

- Plant some very tall and fast-growing plants, such as maize and sunflowers, so that children can experience their amazing growth from tiny seed to a plant taller than the tallest adult. Lettuce grows so quickly that the whole growing cycle can be witnessed in just a few weeks.
- Make a mathematical landscape by planting bulbs in groups and at different heights: growing provides a huge number of other possibilities for building mathematical concepts and language.
- Stepping-stone pathways through the plants will draw children in, allowing them to have closer contact.

Equipment and resources for growing and investigating wildlife

Although plants and wildlife will be in many parts of your outdoor space, equipment for gardening and wildlife-watching activities is best located in one well-organised and accessible place, perhaps near to any main growing area. A potting shed will have great appeal, will support gardening work in all weather conditions and may spark off associated imaginative play (such as Percy the Park Keeper's cabin or Jack and the Giant's castle). Remember that if children can play in it, this will affect what you can store in it. Equipment needs to have

Figure 3.4 Children are tuned to the fascination and detail of such ordinary things as grass flowers.

designated places so that everyone knows where to find things as they need them. A wooden baton screwed to a nearby wall could provide a place to hook wheelbarrows and other tools. Silhouettes painted onto a wall behind hooks will indicate to children where they should return tools to (and naturally include mathematical matching and calculating experiences). Teach children to clean tools before returning them to storage as they will keep longer and are much nicer for the next person to use: children will enjoy washing them too. Once again, involving children in setting up the organisation of resources and their maintenance creates an abundance of relevant and meaningful learning opportunities, gives children a profound sense of responsibility and belonging, and aids use of resources and their tidying away.

Pesticides and herbicides are dangerous in an early years setting and are neither appropriate nor necessary. There is so much more to be learned from the incidence of pests: imagine the drama of a ladybird eating blackfly on the runner beans, and slugs are the most fascinating of creatures! There are many manual and organic methods that will limit pests enough for a suitable crop, and the effects 'pests' have are all part of discovering the living world. Try to make your gardening as wildlife friendly as possible and use every chance to help children learn how they can take care of their planet.

Figure 3.5 Intimate contact with living things in the natural world.

Resources for growing and investigating

Protective clothing, including child-sized gloves for those who cannot or do not want to have direct contact with soil

Water supply – water butt or outdoor tap (make the most of collected rain water and previously used 'grey' water)

Hose and attachments

A good range of watering cans of different sizes and spouts

Large and small buckets with handles

Long-handled spades, forks, rakes, brooms (most child-sized with one or two adult-sized)

Child- and small adult-sized hand tools (metal are more effective than plastic, but they do rust if not kept clean). Try to buy good quality specialist children's tools.

Wheelbarrows – have several as these will be very popular

Biodegradable pots and seed trays (or use recycled margarine pots, etc.) – a variety of sizes increases mathematical potential

Hanging baskets and brackets, a wide variety of interesting containers

Peat-free compost and loam topsoil, large trugs with lids for storage, scoops

Landscape (weed control) fabric and mulches (bark, pebbles, slate, etc.)

Canes (tape the ends to protect eyes), twine, plant markers, waterproof pens

Wood for making homemade plant markers at the woodwork bench

Plant feed, water-holding granules – buy containers with childproof lids and store out of reach

A selection of baskets for carrying and transporting seeds, cut flowers, crops, etc.

Mat and broom to limit mud taken indoors

Sink or washing-up bowl with warm soapy water for hand-washing

Soapy water, scrubbing brushes and old towels for cleaning tools before storing

Collecting pots and good-quality A5 sheet and hand-held magnifiers to look closely at mini-beasts. Bug viewers that both contain and magnify are best – some allow above and below viewing

A small microscope is a great addition; digital versions are available from main educational suppliers

Telescope and binoculars for watching birds; nest box webcams are available but expensive

Children's digital cameras and mobile tape recorder

Looking after your plants

When considering what and where to grow in your outdoor space, it is important to factor in how the plants will be looked after. The main workforce for this must be the children, and they will quickly and willingly take on this responsibility, making decisions and leading the way: watering, weeding, keeping an eye out for insects, harvesting, sweeping. As adults, our role is to gently hand over these decisions and tasks while supporting children to be successful enough, to get the most from experiences and to develop feelings of responsibility, ownership, trust and competence. Such experiences also enable children to become aware of cause and effect as they realise the consequences of events in the environment or actions they have (or have not) taken. Think ahead to consider what maintenance will be involved in a project and when things should happen. How about making a calendar of events with the children so they can take charge or let you know when things need doing?

Regular watering is especially important when establishing new plants, through flowering and when fruit is swelling. Plants will weaken if they dry out often or for long, making them susceptible to disease. Conversely, if roots sit for long in waterlogged soil, caused by insufficient drainage and a rainy climate or enthusiastic watering (very likely with young children), your plants will also suffer.

To help the situation during summer holidays, water-holding capacity in containers can be much improved by mixing compost into soil and adding water-holding granules. Spend time with the children examining how these change with water (it is fascinating) and discussing how they might help the plants (but also why they might be dangerous to swallow). Water loss by evaporation (and weed growth) can be substantially reduced by laying landscape fabric over the surface and covering this with a mulch. Garden centres now supply many attractive mulching materials that also make good resources for play: take children to help choose those that will be best in your setting.

Clearly, a good water supply from an outdoor tap or water butt will make growing much more manageable, and wherever possible collect rainwater and use waste water from play. So that water in a water butt does not become a safety hazard, ensure that the lid is well secured at all times and bring children's attention to this issue. It is important to help children understand what a vital, precious and limited resource the world's water is so that they develop habits for its conservation. Let children make decisions about when to water, based on recent weather conditions, and provide a really good supply of watering equipment. As well as watering cans, buckets and a hose, try challenging older children to come up with an irrigation system using guttering and pipes. You could also investigate how a seeper hose operates and see if children can make their own homemade version. Irrigation systems are likely to attract and fascinate children who are interested in how things connect (connection schema).

Small containers soon run out of the minerals and nutrients plants need for healthy growth: enhance levels in the soil when planting and top up with liquid feeds specific to the kind of plant, especially during fruit production (tomatoes especially need this care). Change the soil when replacing plants and give plants a bigger container if they appear to be struggling. For larger containers, wheeled planter stands positioned underneath before filling with soil will allow the plants to be moved to a better location if required.

Figure 3.6 Alongside growing, young children need to simply explore the earth itself.

Getting the most out of growing and the living world with young children

Young children use play to process, practise and experiment with their feelings and understandings of new experiences. It is very important that we plan for plenty of time and opportunities for them to work through all the real and first-hand experiences they are having with plants and living creatures. Although there are many possible follow-up activities, much of this should be through child-initiated and child-directed play. Our role is to find out what has captured interest and to provide a responsive range of play contexts: in addition, much is to be gained by involving the children in setting these up.

Here are some of the ways children might be helped to make deeper sense of all their new experiences:

- Alongside growing, young children need to simply dig in the earth! Try to provide an area of soil which is big enough for children to stand in to use their whole body with long-handled tools (see Chapter 2, 'Providing soil'). As well as just digging, they will also find worms, millipedes and woodlice and be able to mix in water to explore mud. Make sure digging areas are clearly marked out and separated from growing areas so that children can tell where they can dig and where plants are growing, to avoid newly sprouting seeds being dug over!

- Ensure that children have plentiful amounts of time for simply *being* in close and mindful contact with the living world, just wallowing in the sensations and feelings it offers, and being present in the here-and-now moment. This is something that children are naturally good at, but as educators we tend to feel we should be doing something and children should be progressing to 'next steps'.
- Ensure too that children have lots of opportunities and as long as they need to immerse themselves in their fascinations with living things. Simply naming things is nowhere near enough to create deep interest and connection – indeed, suggesting children make up their own names might well be of more value. Joining children in sustained watching, listening and admiring garden birds, small mammals such as squirrels, and mini-beasts – going about their normal behaviour and interactions with each other – will help them to maintain attention, witness far more detail in what they are observing and want to know more about these creatures with whom they share their world.
- Talk with children naturally as much as possible during and after new experiences, making sure you give plenty of time for sharing their fascination and delight: this 'shared thinking' is a very effective way to build understanding. Be careful though to keep on their wavelength and not to intrude on moments that are better without talk!
- Narrative is the way the human brain prefers to make sense of experiences, and children are avid story-makers and listeners. Whenever the right moment arises during real experiences (or afterwards), make up a story, retell a known story and take children's comments as a starting point for verbally building shared stories together – however simple or short that might be. What is important is that this is fun and playful (and remember that it is for deepening learning not for assessment!).
- Take children to visit a garden centre, market, florist or greengrocer as part of the preparations for growing plants, and to give them ideas, roles, material and dialogue for pretend play that follows from planting and harvesting experiences. A simple wooden shed as a basis for such role play will be much more versatile than purpose-made plastic structures.
- Offer children opportunities to re-enact an experience repeatedly, such as burying and uncovering plastic vegetables from the digging area.
- Bury plastic mini-beasts in the digging area (a large container or builder's tray filled with soil makes a suitable alternative) so that children can search for, collect and return them.
- Look for evidence of schematic interests amongst your children and make sure they can further investigate them through activities related to your growing projects by having the right kinds of resources available. Examples

might be burying and covering seeds and bulbs (envelopment); collecting; filling baskets and buckets with soil or produce (containment or enclosure); transporting these in wheelbarrows and with bikes; weaving in and out between tall plants (going through); watering from a watering can or hose (transporting and trajectories). It is very likely that, at any one time, several children will be interested in similar schemas and that they will enjoy playing together because of this.

- Many children will become absorbed with gathering flower heads (dandelions and daisies are favourites) and seeds such as acorns and sycamore helicopters. They will then spend long periods using them in pictures and patterns or may use them to represent other things in their imaginative play. Consider whether it is possible to take children on foraging expeditions where plants grow naturally, such as wild blackberry picking, or to a fruit farm for strawberries.

- Butterfly and ladybird wings can be made by tying lengths of shiny fabric to a child's wrists (soft ponytail bands are ideal for this) so that children can explore what it is like to be a bird or insect on the wing through running, dancing and swirling: this may also develop into fantasy play.

Figure 3.7 Ensure that children have plenty of time to wallow in sensations and feelings.

- Natural-world experiences are likely to inspire creative activity with chalk, paint, weaving or sculpture. To avoid breaking the connection with the stimulus, make sure children can access such resources and express their ideas outdoors as well as inside.
- Help children to become proficient at using a camera so that you can make books to show the sequence of growth of a particular plant, or laminate children's images to make matching and sequencing floor games. Enlarged images could be cut up to make simple puzzles. These can all be very effective ways to allow children to revisit direct experiences in their own time – children will get more out of this if they are supported to make the puzzles themselves.
- Make a collection of fiction and non-fiction books, gardening magazines and catalogues. As evidence of children's abiding interest in the natural world, there are a great many appropriate children's books to share on this theme, so select those that have relevance to the actual experiences your children are having. There are several appropriate themes for homemade story bags with props, such as *Handa's Surprise* (Eileen Brown, 2006) and *Oliver's Vegetables* (Vivian French and Alison Bartlett, 1995), which could be used in a very active way outdoors.
- Because of the central importance of growing food in human lives through the ages, many of our traditional songs and rhymes are associated with growing, the weather, harvesting and the creatures with which we share the world. Try asking parents and grandparents to share favourites from their childhood days, so that children can be part of this heritage and learn rhymes from around the world.
- Use an area with several containers or other suitable planting to create a cosy spot for quiet play and children's own story-making: provide blankets, relevant books and selected puppets in baskets to make the perfect outdoor book corner. A snack will also taste better outdoors amongst the plants that produced it!
- Small-world resources are invaluable for providing play opportunities to process prevailing interests from real experiences, which might last for quite a while after the actual event. A wheeled trolley with pull-out trays is just the thing for bringing appropriate sets outside as part of the continuous provision, so that children can play out thoughts and feelings as they arise. Provide a core that responds to the interests you predict from your children and be ready to enhance this as you notice additional specific interests.
- This aspect of outdoor provision is filled with appropriate opportunities to help children learn how to keep themselves and others safe. Without worrying or scaring children, utilise their motivation and attention to embed risk awareness and safety knowledge into experiences in a meaningful way. Be prepared to remind children many times though before they automatically use this knowledge.

- Many settings link their indoor and outdoor provision by hatching and keeping caterpillars indoors and then releasing the butterflies into the plants outside. Photographs, information books and computers all provide a wealth of ways to extend direct outdoor experiences and to look for answers to children's endless questions about the living world.

Look deep into nature, and then you will understand everything better.

(Albert Einstein)

Rhymes and songs

A useful website for finding the words of traditional songs and rhymes collected especially for the early years is www.bigeyedowl.co.uk

An Apple a Day
Autumn Leaves
Baa Baa Black Sheep
Chick, Chick, Chick, Chick, Chicken
Cut Thistles in May
Daffy Down Dilly
Dingle Dangle Scarecrow
Falling Leaves
Five Little Peas in a Peapod
Here's the Beehive
Incy Wincy Spider
In Spring I Look Gay
Ladybird, Ladybird
Little Robin Redbreast
Mary Had a Little Lamb
Mary, Mary Quite Contrary
Little Boy Blue
Oats and Beans and Barley Grows
One Potato, Two Potato
The Fly Has Married the Bumblebee
The North Wind Doth Blow
There's a Big Eyed Owl
To Market, to Market

Children's books to support gardening and growing

A Busy Year Leo Lionni (Alfred A. Knopf Books for Young Readers 2004)
★*A Child's Garden: A story of hope* Michael Foreman (Walker Books 2010)
A Dandelion's Life John Himmelman (Children's Press 1999)
A Harvest of Colour Melanie Eclare (Ragged Bears 2005)
A Leaf Can Be . . . Laura Purdie Sala and Violeta Dabija (Millbrook Press 2012)
And the Good Brown Earth Kathy Henderson (Walker Books 2006)

Carrot Soup John Segal (Simon & Schuster 2006)

Christopher Nibble Charlotte Middleton (OUP Oxford 2010)

Dandelion Adventures L. Patricia Kite and Anca Harton (Millbrook Press 1998)

Doing the Garden Sarah Garland (Francis Lincoln Children's Books 2007)

Eddie's Garden and How to Make Things Grow Sarah Garland (Frances Lincoln Children's Books 2006)

From Seed to Dandelion (How Things Grow) Ellen Weiss (Children's Press 2007)

Grandpa's Garden Stella Fry and Sheila Moxley (Barefoot Books 2012)

Grow It! Georgie Birkett (Child's Play International 2009)

Handa's Surprise Eileen Browne (Walker Books 2006)

★How Big is Big? Comparing plants Vic Parker (Heinemann Library 2011)

In the Garden Katy Couprie and Antonin Louchard (Tate Publishing 2004)

Jasper's Beanstalk Nick Butterworth and Mick Inkpen (Hodder Children's Books 2008)

Jim and the Beanstalk Raymond Briggs (Puffin 1973)

Jody's Beans Malachy Doyle and Judith Allibone (Walker Books 2010)

Making Minestrone Stella Blackstone and Nan Brooks (Barefoot Books 2000)

Oliver's Vegetables Vivian French and Alison Bartlett (Hodder Children's Books 1995)

One Child One Seed Kathryn Cave in association with Oxfam (Frances Lincoln Children's Books 2003)

★Plant Life Cycles (Nature's patterns) Anita Ganeri (Heinemann Library 2006)

Rosie Plants a Radish Kate Petty and Axel Scheffler (Macmillan Children's Books 2000)

Secret in the Mist Margaret Nash and Stephen Lambert (Gullane Children's Books 2004)

Seeds (Plants) Patricia Whitehouse (Raintree 2003)

Sunflower House Eve Bunting and Kathryn Hewitt (Voyager Books 1999)

The Dandelion Seed Joseph Antony and Cris Arbo (Dawn Publications 1999)

The Gigantic Turnip (book with CD) Aleksei Tolstoy and Niamh Shark (Barefoot Books 2006)

★The Giving Tree Shel Silverstein (HarperCollins Publishers 1992)

The Pea and the Princess Mini Grey (Red Fox 2004)

The Tiny Seed Eric Carle (Puffin 1997)

Tilda's Seeds Melanie Eclare (Ragged Bears 2006)

★Watch It Grow: Pumpkin Barrie Watts (Franklin Watts 2002)

Gardening magazines with lots of full colour images

Children's books to support mini-beasts and small animals

Bug Books (ladybird; bee; ant; caterpillar; fly; worm; snail; woodlouse; beetle; earwig) Karen Hartley and Chris Macro (Heinemann Library 2006)

Comparing Minibeasts series (minibeast homes; minibeast senses; minibeast bodyparts; minibeast babies; minibeast food; minibeasts on the move) Charlotte Guillain (Heinemann Library 2011)

Creature Comparisons: Birds Tracey Crawford (Heinemann Library 2007)

Ears and the Secret Song Meryl Doney (Williams B. Eerdmans Publishing 1995)

Edward Goes Exploring David Pace (Ladybird Books 1997)

Growing Frogs Vivian French and Alison Bartlett (Walker Books 2008)

If At First You Do Not See Ruth Brown (Red Fox 1983)

Inch by Inch Leo Lionni (William Morrow 1996)

Keeping Minibeasts (spiders; earthworms; slugs and snails) Chris Henwood and Barrie Watts (Franklin Watts 1988)

Lenny in the Garden Ken Wilson-Max (Frances Lincoln Children's Books 2009)

Life as a Butterfly Vic Parker (Heinemann Library 2004)

Nuts to You! Lois Ehlert (Voyager Books 2004)

One Mole Digging A Hole Julie Donaldson and Nick Sharratt (Macmillan Children's Books 2009)

Snail Trail Ruth Brown (Anderson Press 2000)

Tadpole's Promise Jeanne Willis and Tony Ross (Andersen Press 2005)

The Bad-Tempered Ladybird Eric Carle (Puffin Books 2010)

The Birdwatchers Simon James (Walker Books 2002)

The King of Tiny Things Jeanne Willis and Gwen Millward (Puffin 2010)

The Rabbit Problem Emily Gravett (Macmillan Children's Books 2010)

The Very Busy Spider Eric Carle (Puffin 1996)

The Very Hungry Caterpillar Eric Carle (Puffin Books 2005)

Yucky Worms Vivian French and Jessica Ahlberg (Walker Books 2012)

Further information and resources – support organisations

BBC Nature website – www.bbc.co.uk/nature

Garden Organic – dedicated schools website, www.organicgardening.org.uk/organicgardening/schools.php

Growing Schools – dedicated to supporting educators to use the outdoors across the curriculum, www.growingschools.org.uk/earlyyears

Learning through Landscapes can give a wide range of support through its early years supporters and membership schemes, www.ltl.org.uk

Nurture Store website and *Nurture Store Facebook page* have a wealth of ideas and comments about rich experiences of the garden and living world, http://nurturestore.co.uk/category/school-gardening-club and www.facebook.com/NurtureStore

Royal Horticultural Society website for huge amounts of advice, including advice on potentially harmful garden plants, www.rhs.org.uk/Gardening, and pages specifically for children and families, www.rhs.org.uk/children

Royal Society for the Protection of Birds (RSPB) – www.rspb.org.uk/youth/learn/earlyyears

World Wildlife Fund (WWF) – www.wwf.org.uk

Further information and resources – suppliers

Ernest Charles – suppliers of wildlife-related products, www.ernest-charles.com

Gardening tool range for early years from NES Arnold, www.nesarnold.co.uk

Hens for Hire – school hen-keeping specialists who hire out eggs, incubators, chicks and hens, and supply support, training, resources and (importantly) holiday care, www.hensforhire.co.uk

Insect Lore – suppliers of insects and related educational resources, www.insectlore-europe.com

Mindstretchers – for garden and discovery resources, www.mindstretchers.co.uk

Muddy Faces – for enhancing the wildlife value of your outdoor area, good-quality gardening equipment and living world resources, www.muddyfaces.co.uk (under 'Early Years', 'Gardening')

Naturescape – wildflower farm catalogue, advice and free visits (Nottinghamshire), www.naturescape.co.uk

Reflections on Learning – for enhancing the wildlife value of your outdoor area, garden and discovery resources and fast-growing vegetable seed packs, www.reflectionsonlearning.co.uk

RSPB shop (http://shopping.rspb.org.uk) and *Cosy* (www.cosydirect.com) supply nest box web-cameras

Wiggly Wigglers – for organic and wildlife gardening products, www.wigglywigglers.co.uk

Further information and resources – gardening books

101 Kid-Friendly Plants: Fun plants and family garden projects Cindy Krezel (Ball Publishing 2007)

Edible Schoolyard: A universal idea Alice Waters (Chronicle Books 2009)

Every Nursery Needs a Garden: A step-by-step guide to creating and using a garden with young children Ann Watts (David Fulton Publishers 2011)

Gardening with Children Beth Richardson (Taunton Press 1998)

Gardening with Children Kim Wilde (Collins 2007)

Get Set Go! Sustainability: A step-by-step guide to creating a sustainable early years setting Anthony David (Practical Pre-School Books 2010)

Grow It, Eat It: Simple gardening projects and delicious recipes Dorling Kindersley (Dorling Kindersley 2008)

Kids in the Garden: Growing plants for food and fun Elizabeth McCorquodale (Black Dog Publishing 2010)

My Favourite Colour is Green: Inspiring children to care for their planet Pre-school Learning Alliance (Pre-school Learning Alliance 2010)

Planning for the Early Years: Gardening and growing Alistair Bryce-Clegg and Jennie Lindon (Practical Preschool Books 2012)

RHS Grow Your Own for Kids! Chris Collings and Lia Leendertz (Mitchell Beazley 2012)

RHS Ready, Steady, Grow Royal Horticultural Society (Dorling Kindersley 2010)

Roots, Shoots, Buckets & Boots: Activities to do in the garden Sharon Lovejoy (Workman Publishing 1999)

Sunflower Houses: Inspiration from the garden Sharon Lovejoy (Workman Publishing 2001)

The Early Years Gardening Handbook Sue Ward (Practical Pre-School Books 2010)

The Garden Classroom: 52 kids gardening activities for art, craft, science, maths, literacy and play Cathy James (Nurture Store 2012) – superb, colour photograph-illustrated e-book, purchasable as a PDF from www.nurturestore.co.uk

The Languages of Food: Recipes, experiences, thoughts Reggio Children (Reggio Children 2008)

The Little Book of Growing Things Sally Featherstone (Featherstone Education 2003)

The Wonder of Trees: Nature activities for children Andrea Frommherz and Edith Biedermann (Floris Books 2012)

Why Dirt Is Good Mary Ruebush (Kaplan Publishing 2009) – a very accessible explanation of how beneficial germs support the development of a healthy immune system

Further information and resources – mini-beasts and small animals

Butterfly: A photographic portrait – a treasure trove of stunning large-format, close-up photography of caterpillars and butterflies from around the world by Thomas Marent (Dorling Kindersley 2008)

Garden Bird Songs and Calls – 60 minutes of CD recordings by Geoff Sample (Collins 2009)

Guide to the Top 50 Garden Birds Field Studies Council (Field Studies Council 2010)

How to Make a Wildlife Garden Chris Baines (Frances Lincoln 2000)

Ideas for Bird Feeders – there are several useful collections of ideas for bird feeders at https://pinterest.com (search under 'bird feeders')

Minibeasts and More: Young children investigating the natural world Ros Garrick (British Association for Early Childhood Education 2006)

Nano Nature: Nature's spectacular hidden world – another fabulous reference book of large format, very close-up images to delight and intrigue children with the miniscule, by Richard Jones (Collins 2008)

RHS Wildlife Garden: Simple wildlife-friendly activities Martyn Cox (Dorling Kindersley 2009)

RSPB Big Garden Birdwatch – annual family and schools event for the last weekend (for families) or week (for schools) in January, www.rspb.org.uk/birdwatch and www.rspb.org.uk/schoolswatch

The Garden Bird Survival Guide David Cromack (Ringpress Books 1999)

The Little Book of Living Things Linda Thornton and Pat Brunton (Featherstone Education 2005)

The Little Book of Mini Beast Hotels Ann Roberts (Featherstone Education 2011)

Summary

- Grow plants wherever you can in your outdoor space. Contact with the natural world through living things and growing plants is essential for young children's well-being and emotional development. The natural world takes care of children and we must help them take this with them through their lives.
- Growing vegetables and fruit and eating the products contributes to young children's physical health through exercise and diet, and their mental health through building a sense of wonder, belonging and harmony with the natural world. Growing can give children lifelong interests and healthy lifestyle habits.
- The natural world provides a fantastic stimulus for communication as children very much want to share their discoveries. Learning potential is rich in every aspect of the curriculum.
- Slow right down to make the most of every opportunity: there is so much potential in every step of the growing process and every interaction with the living world.
- Adults do not need to be experts but they do need to be facilitators. It is more fun and learning together is a highly effective teaching strategy.

- There is a huge amount of help available. Take horticultural and wildlife projects a little step at a time, allowing your confidence to grow.
- Let children give the lead to developments wherever possible, harnessing their enthusiasm and desire to interact with and know about living things, paying close attention to what it is that interests them, and negotiating a curriculum that is emergent rather than pre-planned.
- Families have a lot to offer settings starting out with growing. This theme is a very effective way for parents/carers to become involved in their children's learning, both in the setting and at home.
- Make the most of your locality to bring children into contact with the natural world all through the year. For example, acorn and conker collecting hold a deep fascination, and playing in huge piles of accumulated leaves in the park may not be easy to provide within the setting.
- Emphasise relaxation, pleasure, wonder, joy and the aesthetics of being in contact with the living world. Each child will respond and interact differently, yet this will contribute to long-term well-being at a deep level within every individual.
- Aim to lay the foundations for a caring approach to the planet with an abiding desire to spend time in it and find out more about it.

Chapter 4

Providing for physical play and movement outdoors

What this chapter is about

- Why do young children need movement play?
- What do movement and physical activity do for young children?
- What movement experiences do young children need in their outdoor play?
- Providing opportunities for the full range of physical and movement experiences

  - Features to encourage movement and physical activity
  - Good resources for physical play and what children might do with them

- Health and safety considerations – managing risk; providing challenge
- Children's books, rhymes and music
- Further information and resources

We think in all the ways we experience . . .

It amazes me how quickly and how often we forget that we are embodied, that we see the world the way we do because we live in these bodies. . .
(Sir Ken Robinson, *The Element*, 2009; TED talk, 2012)

Why do young children need movement play?

Young children absolutely love to move and are driven to develop their physical abilities from birth onwards. They also have great motivation to join in with others, both children and adults, and older children are a great stimulus for younger ones. This drive for movement is perhaps so strong because of its fundamental influence on all other aspects of a child's life, but modern life is not conducive to giving children anywhere near enough of the physical experiences they must have for health and happiness, now and in their futures. Early years settings play an increasingly important role in giving children both the amount of movement and the range of physical experiences they need, and the outdoor space can be a highly effective place to provide this.

For most settings, activities for physical development already form one of the main uses of the outdoor space, recognising the greater freedom and stimulus this environment offers. However, as effective practitioners we must really explore what young children gain from movement and why, so that we can broaden and deepen provision in this area to fully meet developmental needs across all aspects of physical, emotional and mental health, and recognise the central role of movement in brain-building and learning. It is vital that we offer children lots of time and lots of movement experiences, and it is also important that we work with the child's own drives and interests, that they move forward at their own pace and that all physical experiences are enjoyable and full of play. Young children seem to intuitively know what their body needs, and it is the child's joy and satisfaction in movement that is our purpose and our delight to witness.

Take a little time now to remember what physical experiences you loved and sought out when you were young: getting giddy, walking along walls and jumping off, climbing high so you could see 'forever', swings and see-saws, practising handstands and cartwheels, hanging upside down, walking backwards, skipping with friends, rough and tumble play with siblings. All these had significance for the development of your growing brain and sensory systems, which is probably why you enjoyed them and wanted to engage in them over and over again. Young children are developing a vast array of physical abilities at a pace that is never matched in later life: 50 per cent of a child's learning happens in the first five years. 'Inefficient movement' is harder to rectify later than other kinds of learning delays, and movement itself affects so much else about children's development, not least their self-image and feelings of self-worth.

Figure 4.1 Young children absolutely love to move.

What do movement and physical activity do for young children?

Through playful movement and physical activity the child can explore who they are, how the world works and how they fit into it. Through movement the young child can get a real sense of their own body and derive great pleasure in mastering new abilities – and experience considerable frustration and determination in getting there! They can also work out how to operate in a world full of gravity and objects. Movement seems to play a big role in building relationships, starting with being rocked by a parent or carer and developing into active play with other children who become friends. A close look at the roles movement and action play shows just how important this aspect of provision is.

Mental health through the joy of movement

- Children enjoy the feeling of their body, and what it can do gives feelings of pleasure.
- Movement actually makes the brain feel alert and energised through the production of positive chemicals – giving the feeling of 'life in every limb'.
- Mental well-being develops through experiencing the joy of moving, and from satisfying the strong urge to explore movement and extend capabilities.
- Self-image, self-confidence and feelings of efficacy grow through mastering new abilities, especially when others show that they value these (perhaps this is why young children constantly ask us to 'look at me').
- A love of activity and movement provides emotional benefits throughout life.

Physical health through activity

- Activity helps the body develop muscles, ligaments, tendons, bones, nerve connections, and heart and lung function – and therefore strength, agility, flexibility and fitness.
- Movement builds the sensory pathways and nerve centres in the brain that coordinate and execute the vast array of movement and control skills needed for life.
- Young children are concentrating on developing a sense of their body and its position in space, in relation to gravity and other objects.
- Development of the trunk, shoulder, elbow and wrist are critical to efficient deployment and functioning of the hand and therefore play a huge role in the development of tool use and handwriting. Development of both strength and delicate, precise control requires a long journey of active experience for the hands themselves too.
- Energy use and controlled weight when young help to prevent obesity and diabetes in later life.

Figure 4.2 Children need endless opportunities to use their limbs, hands and feet.

- Moving well brings enjoyment of being active so that children continue to seek activity, laying foundations for attitudes and interests for an active life as 'runner beans rather than couch potatoes' (Ouvry, *Exercising Muscles and Minds*, 2003)!

Building core neurological sensory systems

- Movement constructs internal sensory systems that give us body awareness, balance, control, coordination and dexterity.
- It helps the brain to function as a whole, with the two hemispheres communicating at high speed so that they can work in an integrated way.
- Moving enables attention and concentration, and supports development of those parts of the brain involved in self-regulation and self-organisation.
- Movement plays a central role in the development of vision – moving in space develops the ability to perceive, interpret and react to the motions of one's own body and of other objects. Moving in three-dimensional space also integrates vision with balance and hearing.
- It develops many aspects of vision important for life functioning and safety, including tracking, binocular vision, depth perception and peripheral vision.

Personal and social health through physical play with others

- Movement and physical competences enable the child to join in with the things their friends enjoy doing.
- They also enable the child to do the things others can do, that are socially valued by peers.
- Movement helps with learning how to play with others; for instance, research suggests that simply running together helps friendships form.
- Many children form relationships through boisterous, physical interactions, such as chasing, rough-and-tumble and being superheroes, and these are popular ways for boys to play. Through this they can learn how to manage emotions, understand limits and develop social understanding and skills.

Learning through doing and moving

- Young children need to move and do in order to learn.
- Development of the brain and the body are completely intertwined and cannot be separated.
- Being active activates the brain to make it attentive and ready for new learning, and increases the involvement of all parts of the brain.

Figure 4.3 Spinning and being upside down are both much loved and neurologically important.

- Movement physically builds the brain through production of a chemical (BDNF) that supports nerve growth and network connections, so that new learning is better laid into memory.
- Concrete experiences sensed with the whole body give fuller meaning and lasting, embodied memories.
- Movement is our first 'language' and remains very important to us both for thinking and for communicating throughout life. We use gesture, facial expression and body posture to convey most of what we mean and how we feel.
- Expressing new understanding through movement deepens the learning.

What movement experiences do young children need in their outdoor play?

Movement and physical activity will be part of nearly everything children do outdoors, as they learn most effectively through doing and moving. We can build upon these desires to maximise the actions and movements that most help physical development. If we know what physical experiences children most need, then we can build these into daily play in *all* areas of provision outside, as well as planning for specific physical activities or having a dedicated area for physical play. It is clear that children need very many opportunities to work on all these areas over time, without rushing them, and this provides a very strong reason why outdoor provision is best available all of the time!

- In order to develop the child's sense of balance and how to cope with gravity, they need very many experiences of moving and being moved in the three planes of space: through twisting, turning, spinning, rolling, rocking, swinging, tilting, tipping, jumping, bouncing, falling, sliding, being upside down and moving fast. These experiences provide the movement sensations required to wire up vestibular organs in the inner ear that tell us where we are in space in relation to the force of gravity. Adults generally do not like these turning and tipping sensations as this system is well developed: children are driven to seek them because it is very important that they develop this sensory system – and they find every opportunity to do so! The vestibular sensory system underpins balance and coordination, and when it is functioning well we feel at ease in our body and are able to control it well. Balance, coordination and control in turn underpin so much else, so this is a hugely important developmental process for all young children.
- To develop an awareness of their body and knowing where their limbs and 'edges' are, children need lots of opportunities for pushing, pulling, stretching, hanging, throwing, lifting and carrying, rough-and-tumble and being wrapped up. These experiences develop nerve sensors in our muscles, joints, ligaments and tendons, wiring them up to the brain so that we can sense every part of our body's position and movement. This vital sensory system,

known as *proprioception* or 'self perception', gives us the ability to perceive (feel) ourselves from the inside so that we can function smoothly in all the thousands of ordinary movement tasks we carry out every day. Even more profoundly, it actually gives us the feeling of having a body and *being in* this body (something we take for granted but actually a vital developmental process). It is through this sensory system that we acquire a physical sense of existence. Children with a well-developed and integrated proprioceptive system have a firm sense of self and function well in daily tasks, and so are able to feel confident in the world.

• In order to develop a good sense of space and binocular vision, so that they can move around with ease and control and develop perceptions of distance (how far away something is) and direction, children need lots of chances to fit their body into spaces and to manoeuvre around and amongst objects, including going up and down steps (judging where to place the feet). These experiences link up knowledge about the body (the body awareness and balance inner senses) with the visual sensory system, developing body–eye coordination.

• Movement that alternately uses each side of the body helps to link up the two sides of the brain by developing the bridge of nerves between them, and this is now known to be very important for a wide array of functions (one of which is following lines of text smoothly across the page when reading). In fact, every action and every thought involves areas in both hemispheres of the brain, so it is important that information is communicated rapidly and successfully between them. Children need a huge amount of opportunity and encouragement for being on their tummies, crawling, clambering, climbing, running, skipping, pedalling, using steps, stepping stones, slopes and any other 'cross-lateral' activity, from a few months old until well into the school years.

• For muscle tone and bone density, gross-motor strength, upper-arm strength, control and mobility, fine manipulative strength and dexterity, and being able to judge the right strength for the task, children need endless opportunities to use their limbs, hands and feet, to lift and carry, push and pull, jump and land, grasp and hold, manipulate and manoeuvre, throw and catch. Since bone density is built up through impact, the general knocks and bumps that happen in energetic outdoor play need to be seen as part of healthy development too.

• Being able to move easily through a range of positions, following one move-ment with another (flexibility and agility), moving at the right speed and being able to judge when to start and stop (timing), and being able to make fine adjustments to achieve aim or pick up an object are all advanced phys-ical abilities that depend on masses of opportunity over several years to develop body and spatial sense, balance and coordination, integration of these internal senses with sight, touch and hearing, and development of the brain area that plans and carries out motor activity (this is known as praxis, and dyspraxia means difficulty with motor planning). When we consider how much physical development is taking place in the early years of a child's life, it is not at all surprising to find that children are so driven to move and be active in everything that they do!

- The developing child also needs to be able to spend lots of time moving around a landscape that provides a range of different kinds and qualities of surface. Our increasingly indoor lifestyles mean that young children rarely experience ground that is uneven, non-uniform or unpredictable, or that gives way underfoot. Short and long grass, bumpy pavements, uneven forest floor, loose bark, soft sand and wobbly gravel all provide surfaces that require attention and a moment-by-moment response for every step, especially as the child moves from one kind of surface to another.

- So much information enters the body via the feet, which the child then makes a response to in order to move successfully, that it is worth contemplating why we so often insist that children wear shoes when they are outdoors. Shoes remove the often wonderful sensations that the ground can give to the feet, and also prevent the soles, arches and toes from operating as they are supposed to in locomotion. Having carefully checked the environment for unacceptable hazards, there are likely to be places and times where we can enable children to experience so much more of the world through this highly sensitive, but surprisingly robust, part of their body.

- Resting and relaxation are equally important for physical well-being. Children need to know how to relax, to enjoy being calm and still, and to be able to follow the natural cycles of activity and rest that the young human body needs. For children in early years settings and schools this cycle can happen several times a day, so comfortable and relaxing places are as important to provide as areas for energetic play. Dens are ideal, as are places to lie down to look at the sky or to sit and chat. Do not forget, though, that sitting still to demand is a very advanced activity for the young child's level of balance and control development, and most cannot (and should not) do this for more than a few minutes.

Providing opportunities for the full range of physical and movement experiences

Features for movement and physical play

Space to run without obstruction
A variety of surfaces: soft, hard, loose, uneven or bumpy
Different levels: high up and low down
Gradients: gentle and steep slopes, steps and terraces
Interconnecting pathways with variety and challenge built into them
Raised surfaces to balance along and jump off

Stepping stones: different heights and distances apart

Things to crawl, scramble, clamber and climb over, under and through

Vertical poles and horizontal bars, especially 'monkey bars'

Places to dig and fill: sand, soil, gravel

Vertical surfaces for aiming, bouncing and traversing

A wide variety of wheeled vehicles, including carts and wheelbarrows

Lots of things to lift and carry: some need to be heavy and awkward to manage

Lots of flexibility and opportunity for moving and modifying

Multi-sensory resources that stimulate across the senses and support sensory integration

Comfort and places to retreat from activity and to rest

Figure 4.4 A lot of physical challenge can be offered in a small but imaginative space.

Features to encourage movement and physical activity

The outdoor space offers most for movement and physical development when it has a variety of features that work together to give a really wide range of experiences. While many features will be permanent and fixed, some can also be created from resources to make temporary and moveable features.

• *Firm, even and relatively flat surfaces* offer opportunities for running, for using bikes and a variety of wheeled vehicles and toys, and also for chalking out games, runways or simply a line to balance along. A large area of firm surface is very beneficial in outdoor spaces, but try not to let it dominate your provision; pathways offer a good way to combine hard and soft surfacing.

- *Soft, uneven surfaces*, such as grass, smaller areas of sand and bark, and even muddy spots, will provide for a whole host of other activities; not least, learning how to move on uneven ground, 'on-purpose falling over' and turning on the spot until giddiness makes you fall over.

- *Open areas* allow unobstructed energetic activity without disturbing or knocking into others. Boys especially like to run together or engage in high-energy pretend play with police and baddies or superheroes. An open space encourages movement of all kinds: look for ways for girls to get active too, such as dancing to exciting music.

- *Small spaces*, such as tunnels and hidey-holes in bushes, encourage children to crawl through, hide in and feel how their bodies fit into them. Look for ways of providing small spaces in permanent features, such as the space alongside the shed or underneath a look-out platform, as well as through moveable equipment such as barrels and cardboard boxes.

- *Gradients and different levels* provided by steps, slopes, dips and mounds are wonderful for meeting children's strong interest in going up and down and their love of being 'high up'. Learning to negotiate steps and sloping ground is very important for young children, who may mainly experience flat carpets, pavements and shopping malls away from your setting; so do make the most of any you have or look into how you can create 'hilliness' in your outdoor space. Even a small grassy mound, perhaps with a set of steps in one side, will prove very popular for imaginative as well as movement play. Try digging a dip in a grass surface and making a corresponding mound with what is dug out, so creating a nicely undulating surface. A grassy bank is also excellent for rolling down, as most adults will remember. If you have a sloping bank, make the most if it by creating several different ways of going up and down along its length. The side-by-side contrast in movement experiences and methods will add to the learning value – ask the children to invent their own routes as well.

- Curving or meandering *pathways, tunnels and bridges* entice children to follow them, moving from one place to another and learning how to turn them-selves or their vehicle around bends. You can enhance the physical challenge in permanent pathways by embedding pebbles and other items into them, having sections with a gentle or steep gradient and by including traffic-calming-style bumps. Temporary pathways can be made with chalk markings on a hard surface or by using ropes, cones or other small markers: try bamboo canes pushed into soft grass or sand surface to make an 'in and out' pathway.

- *Stepping stones* stimulate children to find different ways of moving along them, such as jumping, hopping, taking giant steps or going in and out between them. They can be set at different distances and heights and can be repositioned occasionally to offer new challenges; make some wobbly too. There are several resources that can be used by children to make their own stepping-stone challenges: make sure you have suitable items available and that children learn how to use them safely.

- *Low walls* with broad tops are very attractive to children who are developing balance and coordination. Jumping off provides a tipping and falling experience as well as the control needed to land: walls made to gradually gain in height offer increasing challenges for children to set themselves. Nursery pioneer Margaret McMillan considered 'jumping-off points' to be an important thing to provide in the nursery school. As well as making good use of any fixed walls and jumping off places in your space, temporary versions can be made with resources such as milk crates and tyres.
- *Traversing walls*, where handholds used for climbing walls are fixed across a length of wall at a height suitable for young children (footholds need be no more than 20–30 cm above the ground), provide marvellous physical experiences that contribute greatly to balance, to strength in the back, neck, limbs and hands, and to coordination across the two sides of the body. Children will learn to judge their own abilities and to stretch them a little more each time: placement of holds can be matched to the children attending the setting. They should always be fitted by a specialist, but most playground equipment companies can supply and fit them to the standards required.
- *Walls* have many other uses for physical play so try to keep areas clear for use. Chalking markings onto them, or using poster paint, will give you the option to change the design on a daily basis, whereas permanent markings preclude a different use, so do think carefully about any permanent markings or murals you decide to have done. Chalking and painting with water or poster paint is in itself a highly physical activity, where children can work with both arms, work on a large and sweeping scale and work side-by-side or collaboratively. If working directly onto the wall is not feasible, try fixing some large wooden boards or sheets of plastic – even hooking up a plain shower curtain will do! Attaching hooks to the wall will also allow you to hook up baskets as targets for throwing, starting with a large, plastic laundry basket and moving to smaller baskets as children's skills develop.
- *Crawling, scrambling, clambering and climbing* are very good for encouraging coordination of the two sides of the body as the alternate use of left and right helps to strengthen linkage across the two hemispheres of the growing brain. The reaching, stretching, pushing and pulling actions in the arms and legs also help to develop body awareness (proprioception) and there is a variety of pressure on the feet. The best features for these activities will have a lot of inherent variety or can be moved and modified to change the movement patterns children are encouraged to make. Large boulders or tree trunks make clambering features that offer marvellous and irregular opportunities which climbing frames often lack. When looking for a fixed climbing frame, select one that offers opportunities to crawl into, under and through small spaces, places to scramble and climb up and over, and additional parts that can be used to modify the basic structure. Some settings have climbing frames made from a series of tyres, from huge tractor to small car and even motorbike sizes. Nets, tunnels, tyres, barrels and cardboard boxes also entice children to clamber and crawl.

- *Poles and horizontal bars* help children to develop their body sense through stretching and hanging, by their arms and perhaps by hanging upside down. When selecting a climbing frame, look for those with opportunity to hang so as to stretch arms and torso and develop grasp and grip; monkey bars are excellent for this even if children cannot bear their own weight for long. Low, horizontal tree branches can be used in this way if there is room for the child to lift their feet off the ground – first check that the branch is sufficiently sturdy. Twisting round a vertical pole while leaning out and doing 'apple turnovers' over a horizontal bar are popular as the turning action also provides vestibular stimulation. Being upside down is very effective for developing the balance system, so do look at ways for children to do this, offering as much support as the child needs. A vertical wooden pole with long ribbons attached can also become a maypole for dancing around.
- *Places to dig* with long-handled tools, such as areas of sand, soil or gravel, provide fabulous physical workouts, especially if they are deep enough to push the spade well under the surface, lift up a full load and transfer it into a waiting container. Young children are very motivated by the possibility of digging a deep hole or trench, and with plenty of wheelbarrows and buckets on hand to fill and push or carry around before emptying them back into the hole, play with such natural materials can provide some of the best opportunities for all-round gross and fine-motor physical development. Filling the hole with heavy buckets of water to create a watercourse continues this satisfying interweaving of intellectual, social, physical and emotional work. Sweeping too holds similar motivation and fascination.
- *Bikes, trikes and other wheeled vehicles* are superb resources for encouraging exactly the kinds of movements and actions that build a child's brain – no wonder children love them so much. They involve pushing and pulling with arms, legs, back and shoulders for development of proprioceptor sensors in muscles, joints and tendons; using both sides of the body alternately for linking up the two sides of the brain; and movements that stimulate the vestibular organs for balance through turning corners and moving fast. Strength, flexibility, hand–eye coordination and timing are also amongst the physical benefits gained from playing with wheeled toys. It is vital, however, to select vehicles carefully, to have a good range, to have good challenges for bike use (such as carrying loads and passengers) and to incorporate bike play into relevant, well-planned and supported role play. Permanent track markings are convenient for adults but lack variety and flexibility of use for children, so do consider making your own to suit the current interests or themes. While bike play can be a repetitive and even disruptive activity, with thought and planning it can become an area of provision full of imaginative and social potential to match what it can offer for physical development.

Figure 4.5 Bikes can do so much for children, socially as well as physically.

Good resources for physical play and what children might do with them

Resources for movement and physical play

Ropes, both long and short, thick and thin
Ribbons, scarves, streamers, fabric strips
Wrist and ankle bells
Music and a CD player
Bubbles, balloons, feathers, leaves to chase
Fabric pieces in a variety of sizes and textures
Large voile scarves, survival blanket (metallic)
Balls, beanbags, pom-poms
Disks, fliers, rings, quoits, hoops
Body ball
Cones
Chalk, foam, water and paint with large brushes
Long-handled brooms, spades and rakes
Baskets, buckets, bags, pulleys
Wheelbarrows
Carts, ride-upons, bikes (especially load or passenger carrying)
Rocking boats and spinning bowls
Pushchairs and prams

Steps and stepping stones, washing-up bowls (strung together)
Small parachute, hammock
Lycra sheet, tunnels
Small soft blankets, cushions, picnic blanket
Milk and bread crates
Logs and branches
Small tyres
Barrels, cardboard boxes and tunnels
A-frames, ladders, planks
Stop watch, egg timer, tape measure

While there are many resources that specifically encourage and support movement and physical play, a lot of the *resources you have for other areas of provision* will also be very good for this: logs and branches from natural materials; crates and large wooden blocks from construction; spades, rakes and brooms from gardening; scarves and fabric from role play. All aspects of outdoor provision also have great potential for giving children the physical experiences they need, so you can capitalise upon this by providing resources that enhance the physical aspect and by encouraging movement as you support the activity. For example, in the sand area, you can set up a pulley system with ropes and buckets, so that children are energetically lifting and pulling heavy weights while they explore sand and play imaginatively. Kitchen utensils can be specially selected for the mud kitchen that provide good physical work for hand development – whisks for turning, spatulas for spreading, mashers for crushing, pestle and mortar for grinding, tongs for squeezing, and so on. Gardening, woodwork and high-energy role play are also full of movement and physical activity: boys especially are drawn to activity and action. Make sure that children who are less physical have opportunities that are attractive to their interests and styles of play, such as offering excellent work for hands, arms, shoulders and torso through washing the windows or cleaning the cars and bikes.

There are also lots of movement activities that simply *make use of the space the child is in*, without needing additional resources: jumping and hopping forwards and backwards; rolling down a slope; playing follow-my-leader; skipping, marching, galloping and chasing; turning on the spot until giddy; twisting around an upright pole; crawling on grass or in sand; puddle-jumping; giant-stepping over cracks; making shadow monsters; chasing feathers or falling leaves; kicking through leaf piles; balancing on low walls; walking on all fours; attempting handstands. These are just a few of the many ideas you and your children will come up with!

Collect a list of *games, action rhymes and songs* with movements that work well outdoors: ask parents for ideas as well as all the staff. Type the lists up as prompt sheets and laminate them, attach a loop to hang them up and keep them to hand outdoors, perhaps on a hook in the shed. This way, you will never be short of ideas and end up using the same old few that you or the children can remember on the spot. Aim to introduce a new game or rhyme each week and use it everyday so that everyone learns it well enough to use it independently: do not forget to add it to the prompt sheets too. Add props for the games to your small physical play resource collection, such as frog-shaped beanbags for a game of *Five Little Speckled Frogs* jumping in and out of a blue laundry basket. Wherever possible get children to move themselves as well, so in this example children might jump with the frog into a chalked-out 'pond'. Chalk is indispensable for marking out spaces, runways, tracks, balancing lines, targets and games – children love to create their own so have plenty of chunky playground chalks. Ropes are highly versatile resources and children will find many ways to use them, such as balancing along a long rope laid on the ground, jumping over a wiggling rope, jumping over or playing limbo under a low rope. Many four- and five-year-olds are ready to try skipping, a marvellously developmental activity: provide plenty of soft, short ropes and suggest activities that build the various skills involved, so as to support persistence. More challenging group and collaborative skipping games, such as '*I like coffee, I like tea, I like ... in with me*', appeal to older children and are superb for developing coordination, communication and social skills – synchronised movement is known to develop friendship and bonding at a deep, subconscious level.

Children love to *dance* and are very responsive to music. Rhythmic movement is an excellent way to make you feel 'in your body' and also to build social relationships by moving in tune with others. Take a transportable CD player outside whenever you can (an external electrical socket is well worth considering, especially in a new build or during refurbishment) so that you can stimulate movement with a wide range of energetic music. It is virtually impossible for a young child not to run in response to *William Tell*, or to twirl to *Carmen*. Irish jigs and samba music will prompt jumping and turning, and African drumming might stimulate stomping and beating. A few simple props, such as ribbons, lengths of floaty fabric and wrist bells, are all you need: attaching ribbons, balloons and scarves to soft pony-tail bands allows children to wear them on their wrists. Larger pieces of see-through material stimulate children to run with the cloth covering their head and arms. As children become familiar with the music, their movement sequences will build in complexity: try videoing the dances and reviewing them with children later on.

There are many resources for children to *push and pull*: bikes, carts, trailers, scooters, pushchairs and prams, brooms, rakes, long-handled spades, wheelbarrows, pulleys and buckets. Children will also make their own resources, such as by threading a rope through a milk crate to pull around. Encourage them to add weight to these so they can experience friction and to attach ropes to wheeled toys so that they can pull each other along. *Lifting, carrying and manoeuvring* with bags, baskets, buckets, watering cans, wheelbarrows and heavy items such as crates, wooden planks, small tyres and logs gives children stretching, coordination and strength-building experiences as well as providing for strong interests in filling, enclosing and transporting. Provide a range of materials to carry, such as

Figure 4.6 The best resources outdoors are large, heavy, awkward and abundant.

sand, pebbles, gravel and water. Den-building, construction, gardening and water play with large resources all involve lots of this kind of physical activity. Make a collection of several types of balls, beanbags and hoops of different sizes, shapes and textures so that children can play with lots of different ways of *throwing, rolling and catching*, gradually building up their skills. By marking on the ground and walls or by providing baskets as targets, children can try all sorts of challenges and games and then invent their own.

Resources such as milk and bread crates and tyres can provide varied opportunities for *balancing, stepping between, bouncing, jumping on and off and teetering* on the edge until you fall off. Provide things to *fit into and crawl through*, such as barrels, tunnels and cardboard boxes. These can also offer *rocking and rolling* experiences for the child inside. Although many early years settings do not have sufficient space for a swing, a hammock can provide a lovely *swinging* sensation, as well as offering a place for relaxation. Staff can also rock children in a blanket or Lycra sheet or with a small parachute. *Tipping, spinning and rocking* are all possible with a spinning bowl, a great item for physical play, available from many educational and special needs suppliers.

Young children have a deep need for *body contact* and a sense of firm enclosure or containment, for physical as well as psychological development. Provide soft sheets, blankets and fabric pieces that children can wrap around their bodies and small places they can climb into, such as cardboard boxes, barrels and tunnels. Play games with Lycra sheets, small parachutes or carpet off-cuts where children are enclosed and gently rolled around according to their own requests (ensure their heads are not covered). This is best done with an adult and just one or two children and for a short duration, so that close attention is given to what the individual child is comfortable with – some children love this kind of experience. Suitably sized body balls can also provide body contact with movement. As a team, discuss your approach to roly-poly play (rough-and-tumble) and other forms of more vigorous physical contact (with adults as well as between children): it has an important developmental role in all social animals, including young humans, and can play a part in your provision for physical play when managed well.

Remember that *enthusiastic, playful adults* can make the best resources! Noticing what the child likes to do and taking the child's lead are the best starting points; children really value your attention and involvement and are also often keen to be given new ideas for play. Encourage children's own exploration and creativity in the ways they use the features and resources, and pick up on a child's idea to introduce a group to a new way of playing with them. Some children, who may have become timid and risk averse, will need sensitive support to help them face appropriate risk and challenge positively. Observe and listen closely; plan to enhance and extend as the children seem ready, but remember how much repetition matters too.

Encourage interaction, talk and collaboration, introducing the *vocabulary of movement* with both useful and interesting words, such as slither, gallop and pounce. Giving children the words that describe body movements, actions and positions does more than helping to increase their verbal vocabulary. When they hear and learn words relating to their own movements, actions and positions, it has personal meaning – and having the verbal word helps them to think about what they are doing more consciously. With this extra support, they are actually more able to think about and plan a sequence of movements and find it easier to carry out such a sequence. The language of movement could relate to several dimensions, and each of these has great application in other areas of learning:

- Position, space and perspective – such as 'up, down, under, over, above, sideways, through, beneath, in, out, between, upside down, fit, put, place'.
- Movement type – such as 'strong, firm, gentle, light, heavy, stretch, floppy, tense'.
- Action – such as 'tap, skip, jump, kick, hop, slide, gallop, slither, squirm, fall, bounce, swing, push, pull, reach'.
- Hand action and manipulation – such as 'prod, poke, squeeze, grasp, grip, pull, twist, pat, smooth, stroke'.
- Interaction – such as 'follow, lead, copy, imitate, hug, stroke, smile'.
- Speed and time – such as 'fast, slow, rapid, meandering, short, long'.
- Sequence – such as 'after, before, when, if, first, then, start, end, finally'.

The language that describes movement is fascinating to children. They will always be motivated to learn words that describe what they and their friends are doing, as this is such a personal and interesting area for them – and this is a perfect example of 'active learning'. Make sure, however, that this language fits in naturally as part of the overall experience and is not forced in any way. This is also a great context for introducing unusual and interesting words. Just as children so often love to learn the names of dinosaurs, they are intrigued by new words such as 'squirm' and 'rapid' or even (for older children) 'meandering' and 'undulating' when they are used in a situation that makes sense and has personal meaning for them. Children should be encouraged to experiment and play with this movement language, perhaps making up words of their own, and this will also encourage them to play and be inventive with movement itself.

Children's love of movement and physicality can also be well supported by the extensive range of *picture books* now available (see the lists of children's books at the end of this chapter). Harness their enthusiasm for sharing a good book by selecting some that respond to their existing physical interests, recognising and valuing the activities they are currently interested in and using the story or images to extend ideas, language, imagination and creativity. Books are also a great way to stimulate new interests or to encourage children to use their developing skills in further ways. The very best books of all, though, are the home-produced ones made in the setting by photographing children's active play: get the most from this by helping children turn these into sequences telling their own stories about what they were doing.

Health and safety considerations – managing risk; providing challenge

Physical play may feel as if it is full of safety problems as children seek to find challenge and develop their abilities beyond current competencies. The outdoors is a much safer place for movement than indoors because inside tends to be full of objects and obstacles; many settings actually report lower accident figures outside than inside. The turning point comes when practitioners view the outdoors as a place where children can learn *how to keep themselves safe* through becoming able to recognise and identify potential harm and knowing how to deal with it. They can also learn how to cope with minor incidents, such as a graze, and come to know that the pain is temporary and will go away. It is through such minor knocks and bruises that children learn about hazards and become aware enough to avoid them next time. Children must have challenge that is developmentally appropriate and they must be willing to make attempts, experience failure and frustration, and develop the determination to succeed – followed in due course by the internal reward of success and the pleasure of feeling capable and competent. These are all important life skills and to deny them to children is a serious mistake with long-lasting effects. Encouraging such a 'growth mindset' through playful physical experiences helps to nurture a child who is resilient, confident and self-assured, and one who is able to embrace life with enthusiasm.

Figure 4.7 Make sure there is always the opportunity for running and chasing.

Safety of children outdoors is paramount and our task is to ensure that children have challenge and freedom within a framework of security and safety; that is, an environment that is safe enough, rather than one completely without risk. Most activities that young children do outdoors in early years settings are highly valuable for all-round development and are not likely to involve significant hazards or harm. However, it is vital that we are fully aware and alert, and use thorough risk management processes to enable such beneficial experiences in a sufficiently safe way. We need to assess potential risks and manage them so that children do have the experiences they need without the possibility of serious harm (this process is known as 'benefit–risk assessment').

A positive approach to risk management will include these steps:

- Check the outdoor area, its features and resources routinely and frequently, removing damaged items or preventing access: repair or replace as soon as possible.
- All adults should observe and interact with children's use of features and resources. Assess benefits and risks constantly, and make adjustments moment-by-moment as they are necessary.
- Know your children – assess the risks for your particular children and try to enable creative physical play rather than limiting opportunities.

- Use your knowledge of physical development to understand what children are seeking to do in their play and identify the benefits of this experience. Knowing how much is being gained, wherever possible, find a way of doing it that is safe enough rather than preventing it.
- Have frequent conversations to review your overall approach to challenge, risk and safety and concerning any specific situations as they arise. Ensure that everyone feels well informed, confident and fully supported. It is vital that challenge and safety is a whole-team approach.
- Teach children how to keep themselves safe in physical activities such as climbing – they need to become aware of hazards and risks so that they can learn to manage them safely.
- Help children become aware of the impact of their own actions on others – this will help them learn to look out for other children's well-being too.

Children want space at all ages. But from the age of one to seven, space, that is ample space, is almost as much wanted as food and air. To move, to run, to find things out by new movement, to feel one's life in every limb, that is the life of early childhood.

(Margaret McMillan, *The Nursery School*, 1930)

Rhymes and music

Everybody Says Sit Down!
Five Fat Peas in a Peapod Pressed
Five Little Monkeys Jumping on the Bed
Five Little Speckled Frogs
Head, Shoulders, Knees and Toes
Here We Go Round the Mulberry Bush
Hickory Dickory Dock
Humpty Dumpty
If You're Happy and You Know It
I'm a Little Indian
In and Out the Dusty Bluebells
One Elephant Went out to Play
Pop Goes the Weasel
Ride a Cock Horse to Banbury Cross
Ring Around the Roses
Round and Round the Garden
Row, Row, Row Your Boat
Ten in the Bed
The Animal Boogie
The Grand Old Duke of York
The Hokey-Cokey
This is the Way the Lady Rides
This Way, that Way, over the Deep Blue Sea
Walking Through the Jungle

There are many types and pieces of music that work very well outdoors; here are some
  examples:
Bolero (Ravel)
Carmen (Bizet)
Carmena Burana (Carl Orff)
Carnival of the Animals (Saint-Saens)
The Flight of the Bumblebee (Rimsky-Korsakov)
The Ride of the Valkyries (Wagner)
The William Tell Overture (Rossini)
African drumming
Bangra music
Irish and Scottish jigs
Salsa music

Children's books about being physical

Around the World: Bicycles Kate Petty (Frances Lincoln with Oxfam 2006)
Around the World: Playtime Kate Petty/Oxfam (Frances Lincoln Children's Books 2007)
Hands Can (Big Book) Cheryl Willis Hudson and John-Francis Bourke (Candlewick Press
  2012)
Let's Play (Window on the world) Paul Harrison (Zero to Ten 2010)
Look What Feet Can Do (Look what animals can do) D.M. Souza (Lerner 2008)
Mrs Armitage on Wheels Quentin Blake (Red Fox 1999)
Over, Under & Through Tana Hoban (Aladdin Books 2008)
Pulls (How things move) Sarah Shannon (Heinemann Library 2009)
★*Push and Pull (Rookie Read-about science)* Patricia J. Murphy (Children's Press 2002)
★*Push and Pull (Science corner)* Angela Royston (Wayland 2012)
Push and Pull (The way things move) Lola M. Schefer (Capstone Press 2000)
Pushing and Pulling (How do things move?) Sue Barraclough (Heinemann Library 2006)
Rabbit and the Big Red Scooter Mark Chambers (Templar 2011)
Scaredy Squirrel Melanie Watt (Happy Cat Books 2007)

Children's books to support movement and physical play

★*A Very Proper Fox* Jan Fearnley (HarperCollins Children's Books 2006)
Ants in Your Pants! Julia Jarman and Guy Parker-Rees (Orchard 2011)
Bumpus Jumpus Dinosaurumpus! Tony Mitton and Guy Parker-Rees (Orchard Books 2003)
Down by the Cool of the Pool Tony Mitton and Guy Parker-Rees (Orchard Books 2002)
Farmer Joe and the Music Show Tony Mitton and Guy Parker-Rees (Orchard Books 2009)
Football Feet Sandra Gilbert Brug and Elisabeth Moseng (Simon & Schuster 2003)
Football Fever Alan Durant and Kate Leake (Macmillan Children's Books 2006)
Giraffes Can't Dance Giles Andreae and Guy Parker-Rees (Orchard Books 2001)
Harris Finds His Feet Catherine Rayner (Little Tiger Press 2009)
Hurry Up and Slow Down Layn Marlow (OUP Oxford 2009)
Mr Strongmouse and the Baby Hiawyn Oram and Lynne Chapman (Orchard Books 2006)
Noisy Parade: A hullabaloo safari Jakki Wood (Frances Lincoln Children's Books 2002)

Pass It Polly Sarah Garland (Frances Lincoln Children's Books 2009)

Saturday Night at the Dinosaur Stomp Carol Diggory Shields and Scott Nash (Walker Books 2008)

Spookyrumpus Tony Mitton and Guy Parker-Rees (Orchard Books 2005)

Swing! Mick Inkpen (Hodder Children's Books 2000)

The Dance of the Dinosaurs Colin and Jacqui Hawkins (HarperCollins Children's Books 2002)

The Dancing Tiger Malachy Doyle, Steve Johnson and Lou Fancher (Simon & Schuster 2005)

★*The Frog Ballet* Amanda McCardie (Red Fox 1997)

The Jungle Run Tony Mitton and Guy Parker-Rees (Orchard Books 2012)

★*The Moon Jumpers* Janice May Udry and Maurice Sendak (Red Fox 2002)

Walking Through the Jungle Julie Lacome (Walker Books 1995)

Where the Wild Things Are Maurice Sendak (Red Fox 2000)

Children's books to support action rhymes and games

Bearobics Vic Parker and Emily Bolam (Hodder Children's Books 1996)

Doing the Animal Bop Jan Ormerod and Lindsey Gardiner (OUP Oxford 2005)

Five Little Monkeys Zita Newcome (Walker Books 2003) – contains over 50 action and counting rhymes, many of which can be used on an active scale outside

Hand, Hand, Fingers, Thumb Al Perkins and Eric Gurney (Random House 1997)

Hand Rhymes Marc Tolon Brown (Turtleback Books 1999)

International Playtime: Classroom games and dances from round the world Wayne E. Nelson and Henry Glass (Fearon Teacher Aids 1992)

Over in the Clover Jan Ormerod and Lindsey Gardiner (OUP Oxford 2009) – this has lots of delightful actions

Over in the Meadow: A counting rhyme Louise Voce (Walker Books 1999) – there are many versions of this book; select one with lots of actions or make your own up!

Rumble in the Jungle (book and CD) Giles Andreae and David Wojtowycz (Orchard Books 2006)

The ABC of Nursery Rhymes Lynne Chapman (Chicken House 2008)

The Animal Boogie: A Barefoot singalong Debbie Harter (Barefoot Books 2011)

The Animal Bop Won't Stop Jan Ormerod and Lindsey Gardiner (OUP Oxford 2011)

The Dancing Dragon Marcia Vaughan and Stanley Wong Hoo Foon (Mondo Publishing 1996)

The Little Dog Laughed: And other nursery rhymes from Mother Goose Lucy Collins (Puffin 1995)

Toddlerobics Zita Newcombe (Walker Books 1997)

Todderobics Animal Fun Zita Newcombe (Walker Books 2000) – although written for toddlers, this is good for children aged 2–3 years

Twiddling Your Thumbs: Hand rhymes Wendy Cope and Sally Kindberg (Faber & Faber 1992)

Walking Through the Jungle: A Barefoot singalong Stella Blackstone (Barefoot Books 2011)

We're Going on a Bear Hunt Michael Rosen and Helen Oxenbury (Walker Books 2009)

We're Going on a Lion Hunt David Axtell (Macmillan Children's Books 2000)

Whoosh Around the Mulberry Bush Jan Ormerod and Lindsey Gardiner (OUP Oxford 2007)

Wiggle and Roar! Rhymes to join in with Julia Donaldson and Nick Sharratt (Macmillan Children's Books 2005)

Further information and resources – background reading

Big Body Play: Why boisterous, vigorous and very physical play is essential to children's development and learning Frances M. Carlson (National Association for the Education of Young Children 2011)

Managing Risk in Play Provision: Implementation guide (DCSF 2008) – the core document describing and explaining the current official approach to 'benefit–risk assessment' by Play England and the Play Safety Forum, available as a free download from www.play-england.org.uk (under 'Resources')

Moving Smart – blog site by Gill Connell, child development expert with a focus on development through movement, movingsmartblog.blogspot.co.uk

The Barefoot Book: 50 great reasons to kick off your shoes Daniel Howell (Hunter House 2010)

The Out-of-Sync Child: Recognising and coping with sensory processing disorder Carol Stock Kranowitz (Skylight Press 2005)

The Well-Balanced Child: Movement and early learning Sally Goddard-Blythe (Hawthorne Press 2005)

Too Safe For Their Own Good? Helping children learn about risk and life-skills Jennie Lindon (2nd edition, National Children's Bureau 2011)

Further information and resources – ideas and planning

Classic Playground Games: From Hopscotch to Simon Says Susan Brewer (Remember When 2008)

Early Movers: Helping under 5s live active and healthy lives – pack from the British Heart Foundation (2012), available as a free PDF or hard copy for £15 donation from www.bhf.org.uk (search under 'Publications')

Encouraging Early Sport Skills Jake Green and Sandy Green (Step Forward Publishing 2008)

Running & Racing (Key issues) Lynne Garner (Featherstone Education 2005)

The Art of Roughhousing: Good old-fashioned horseplay and why every kid needs it Antony Debenedet (Quirk Books 2001)

The Little Book of Dance Julie Quinn and Naomi Wager (Featherstone Education 2004)

The Little Book of Parachute Play: Making and using parachutes in the Foundation Stage Claire Beswick (Featherstone Education 2003)

The Little Book of Playground Games: Simple games for out of doors Simon MacDonald (Featherstone Education 2004)

The Out-of-Sync Child Has Fun: Activities for kids with sensory processing disorder Carol Stock Kranowitz (US Imports 2006)

The Sounds of Leaping – DVD telling the story of how children's enthusiasm for leaping is used to create a symphony by Sightlines Initiative, www.sightlines-initiative.com (online store under 'Videos and DVDs')

Further information – organisations and suppliers

Active Matters – specialist training in physical development in the early years from Dr Lala Manners, www.activematters.org

Choosing Safe Trikes – information sheet from Community Playthings, www.community-playthings.com/c/resources/articles/index.htm (July 2009 newsletter: Outdoor play)

Community Playthings – supplies an excellent range of collaborative wheeled vehicles and carts, www.communityplaythings.co.uk

Jabadao – the National Centre for Movement, Learning and Health offers specialist training and resources for movement in the early years, www.jabadao.org

Knock on Wood – a superb online catalogue of world music and instruments, www.knock-onwood.co.uk

Playtimes: A century of children's games and rhymes is a marvellous collection made by the British Library, including short video clips with children explaining how to play, www.bl.uk/playtimes

Spacekraft – sensory products and equipment to meet additional needs, www.spacekraft.co.uk

Springy's Resource Bag for Physical Play in the Foundation Stage – a very good-value kit of small resources to support movement and physical play with curriculum materials from Learning through Landscapes (by Jan White), from Davies Sport, www.daviessports.co.uk (product number PDML2623)

Summary

- Young children love to move and are strongly driven to develop their physical abilities. We need to fully appreciate just how important and pervasive movement and action is for young children's holistic development.
- It is most important to understand that physical development comes about through *using* the body – moving the body in space and gravity, feeling the body and all its parts, using the whole body, pushing and challenging the body. It does not come about through being still, being restricted, being constrained or being prevented!
- In order for children to develop well physically, they need a great many opportunities every single day to play with, explore and experiment with their bodies, the spaces around them and the features, equipment and resources in their environment. This needs to happen naturally and throughout their day, in and out of everything they do, indoors and especially outdoors.
- Physical play contributes to physical, mental and social health and well-being and to learning, and some types of movement have particular developmental importance at this age, such as for balance, body awareness and coordination.
- Share your knowledge and understanding with parents and carers, so that they can appreciate what their child is doing, understand your approach in the setting and better enjoy and support their child's great need for physicality and movement at home.
- Children should be given a great deal of time for movement and physical play outdoors and to have a very wide range of active experiences.

- All aspects of outdoor provision have opportunities for movement and physical activity – make the most of this for active learning, to increase the range of physical experiences and ensure high motivation for movement.
- The outdoor space offers most for movement and physical development when it has a variety of complementary features that work together to give a really wide range of experiences. Provision can be developed gradually so that all kinds of movements are possible in a range of ways.
- Many of the best features, equipment and resources for supporting physical and movement play are those that settings may already have for other aspects of outdoor provision.
- Effective practitioners delight in sharing children's pleasure and joy of movement and being physically active: adults make great resources for children's physical play.
- Adults should work from children's interests and drives. Children can be trusted to set their own challenges. Interaction, observation, assessment and evaluation are vital in order to plan what to provide or encourage next.
- Children's safety is paramount, but children need appropriate challenge within a framework of security in order to build dispositions for a successful life. We must be fully aware of hazards and work to reduce risks, rather than removing beneficial experiences. These are ideal opportunities for helping children learn how to be safe.

Chapter 5

Providing imaginative, creative and expressive play outdoors

What this chapter is about

- What creative and imaginative play does for young children
- Why take creative and imaginative play outdoors?
- Making provision for creative play outdoors

  - Providing for art and mark-making outdoors
  - Providing for weaving and sculpture outdoors
  - Providing for music and dance outdoors
  - Providing for imaginative play, stories and performance outdoors

- Making the most of creative and imaginative play
- Children's books
- Further information and resources

Only as high as I reach can I grow, only as far as I seek can I go, only as deep as I look can I see, only as much as I dream can I be.

(Karen Ravn)

The potential of the child is stunted when the endpoint of their learning is formulated in advance.

(Carlina Rinaldi)

What creative and imaginative play does for young children

Provision for creative play is one of the most important ingredients in the early years since creativity is so fundamental to our lives, both as children and later as adults. Being able to think creatively – analysing a situation and coming up with new ideas or actions – supports the dispositions needed for learning and life: resourcefulness, positive thinking, having a go, experimentation, a positive attitude to 'failure', resilience, persistence, innovation, thinking outside the box and the ability to express thoughts and ideas. Children need to grow up believing that they are creative, being comfortable with uncertainty and happy to work at finding solutions. These are the life skills needed for twenty-first century life, in which change is certain. 'We need children who see the really tough problems as puzzles, and have the tenacity, the creative resources and the creative ability to solve those puzzles' (Gever Tulley, TED talk, 2011).

It is clear that one of the major developments in children's brains from three to seven years of age is the ability to imagine and to use imagination to play with ideas and feelings. Imaginative 'make-believe' play develops the young brain in the areas of abstract and symbolic thought and allows children to replay their experiences so as to process, understand and internalise them. It allows them to take on different ways of behaving so that they can try out roles and ways of interacting; it enables them to explore other people's minds and thoughts, and this in turn underpins the development of empathy and relationship. Imaginative play is very important for emotional well-being, and one of the main ways children interact with each other is through shared pretend play. Their strong motivation for pretending together supports the development of self regulation, since feelings often need to be managed and overcome in order to keep the shared play going. Young children think and communicate best through story and make-believe activity so they access other areas of the curriculum best through this narrative mode.

Figure 5.1 The outdoors encourages children to be imaginative and think creatively.

Imagination and creativity go hand in hand; we need to be able to imagine in our mind's eye in order to come up with new ideas or see new ways of combining existing ideas. The 'impression–expression' cycle enables deeper understanding by allowing the child's mind to process images of new, real experiences through expressing feelings and thoughts in a personal way, without the pressure of an end-product. Playful, imaginative activity is the bedrock of our ability to be spontaneous, creative and expressive.

Creative, aesthetic and expressive play covers a wide range of opportunities and can be part of most experiences – indeed being imaginative and thinking creatively should be a thread through all that children do. It includes mark-making, art, drawing, pattern-making, design, construction, problem-solving, music, dance, performance, make-believe play (including role play and small-world play), story-telling and sharing or reading books. Spontaneous play and expression is made possible through setting up a 'generous' environment with lots of potential, providing rich and open-ended materials with continuous access to resources, being flexible in planning and ensuring that children know what is there and how it can be made use of. The basic materials must be always available as part of long-term planning so that children build up their exploration of them over time, leading to unexpected and innovative, truly creative, use. Shorter-term planning will introduce new contexts, new materials, new skills taught by an adult and new provocations. What these actually are should emerge from watching and listening to the children.

Why take creative and imaginative play outdoors?

The nature of the outdoors gives ways for children to engage with creative play opportunities in ways not really possible indoors, so this aspect of outdoor provision can significantly enhance and extend children's creative experiences. Many children are simply more relaxed outside, finding it a more liberating, flexible and spontaneous play environment. The greater space gives freedom for movement and large-scale working: there is room to work in 3D, with large materials and in groups. There seems to be more freedom for inventiveness and new ideas. The possibility to be active, noisy, multi-sensory and messy responds to the way many boys like to play so it is perhaps not surprising to find that boys engage more with areas of provision they do not tend to use indoors, such as mark-making. The outdoors accommodates children's natural exuberance when playing musical instruments, singing or dancing. There are very many 'sparks' for creativity from the natural world, real experiences and the locality around the outdoor space. There are lots of suitable role-play scenarios that work better outside, where they have greater authenticity and meaning. Literary and numeracy activities should take place outside, associated with active and imaginative play, so that children do not come to see numbers and writing as an indoor 'work' activity rather than a play activity.

If you are looking to develop your outdoor environment, this is an easy and enjoyable place to start and a great way to broaden the curriculum you offer outside. The central objective should be to create the conditions for imagination and creativity: creating places, presenting resources, introducing the provocations or sparks to intrigue and capture interest, and giving enough time for creative play to emerge and grow deep. Creativity will be expressed and engaged in on a personal level and therefore will be different for each individual child. Creative ideas tend to be emergent – they grow slowly out of exploration and play rather than being decided upon and planned out at the beginning; so playfulness and lots of time outside are key. There is potential for creative thinking in all aspects of provision outdoors – inspiration, problem-solving and expression are possible in all sorts of places, so do not limit your developments to special creative 'areas'.

Making provision for creative play outdoors

Because of the potentially chaotic nature of the creative process, it is important to be prepared for mess and disorder, and to be committed to the extra effort involved on the adult's part. A truly creative outdoor environment is more of a work-site than a workshop! To keep this productive, it is most important to have good basic organisation and routines. Organise resources in a way that enables children as well as adults to access what is needed as the need arises. Designate an area in your shed for mobile containers that will be able to take resources to wherever they are needed: trolleys, trays, toolboxes, crates and backpacks are all suitable. Labelling both the container and its location on the shelves will help keep things in order; laminated photographs are easiest and most effective for both. Develop an expectation that children will put things back and be fully involved in the tidy-up; you will need to persist until this routine is well established but older children will be able to guide younger ones. Once again, if children have made the labels and decided where containers should go in the storage, successful tidying up will be much supported. Wheeled trolleys with slide-out plastic trays really help to provide a creative workshop outside. They can be loaded with mark-making resources, paper, joining materials or small-world resources and easily taken to wherever creative activity is taking place.

Protective clothing is vital so that children stay warm and dry while being free to be inventive and get messy all through the year. Provide old clothes or use rain-wear, as aprons will probably not cover enough (legs and feet tend to get messy) and tend to get in the way. Being able to sit, crawl or lie on the ground enables children to make better use of the outdoor environment, and they need to be able to reach, run and jump – waterproof dungarees (with a jacket added in cold weather) seem to be the most effective solution. Be prepared to wash and dry children and to change clothes. Make sure parents know that this will happen and why; if you make the child's learning visible to them, parents will understand the benefits and work with you. Hand-washing will be needed so have a bowl of warm water available: an outdoor sink makes life a lot easier.

Let your ideas for new creative experiences emerge from what you observe children to be interested in. Working from children's interests and ideas leads to high motivation and fuller involvement, and therefore more complex and deeper learning. Be careful not to overwhelm with too many possibilities and make lots of room for repeating the familiar, while every so often introducing something new. The best learning occurs when the two halves of the early years environment join up. Take some indoor resources outside, bring the stimulus of outside indoors and work across the two using what is different about the outdoors, such as the opportunity to continue on a bigger scale. Experiences outside will spark ideas inside and vice versa.

Providing for art and mark-making outdoors

Resources for art and mark-making outdoors

Trolleys, tool boxes and other mobile containers for resources (*Open Ends* supplies a mark-making wheelbarrow)
Protective clothing, such as rain-wear
A variety of paper, wallpaper lining roll, newsprint roll
Big plastic sheeting (from DIY store), white or clear shower curtains
Clear market stall cover (from *Muddy Faces*), transparent umbrella
Perspex sheet attached to a wall or mounted in wooden frame (the latter allows working on both sides and more colourful effects)
Polyester/cotton sheets
Open up large cardboard boxes to give a big cardboard canvas
Plywood board painted with blackboard paint (attached to wall or with hooks to hang onto a fence)
Clipboards
Pegs, masking tape, duct tape and string
Pens, charcoal, pencils, small palette sets, pencil crayons, wax crayons (for rubbings), big felt pens
Abundant supplies of chunky and pavement chalks, both white and coloured
Thick and thin paint in bottles ready for squirting, spraying or dripping
Shaving foam (for sensitive skin), Gelli Baff, cornflour, soap flakes or other similar material
Non-spill paint pots, spray bottles, squirting bottles
Standard children's paint brushes, down to fine-tipped art brushes (for filigree work)
Bigger decorator's brushes, up to masonry and wallpaper brushes
Large and small emulsion paint rollers (look for variety in DIY stores) and paint tray
A range of sponges in various shapes and sizes
Fly swatters, kitchen brushes, small mops and other utensils as paint applicators
Floor mops and long-handled brooms (child-sized; from *Cosy*)
Writing belts, gardening bags with pockets, tool boxes, caddies and shoe organisers to hold and organise mark-making resources
Natural materials augmented with glass beads, coloured and sparkly items
Recycled materials, such as cardboard boxes and tubes
Magnifiers for close-up observation, A5-sized map-reading sheet magnifier

Viewing frames made from a sheet of card or kitchen/toilet rolls (to focus
   perspectives)
Coloured visors, coloured acetate sheets, safety mirrors
Cameras

Figure 5.2 Use vertical surfaces for mark-making on a grand scale.

Art, mark-making and drawing outdoors

Any outdoor space has lots of potential for working with materials that make
marks in a wide variety of ways. Children can use the ground and surfaces
around the area to work on a big scale with the freedom to be active, messy and
inventive. At the other end of the scale, they will notice the fascinating detail in
things from the natural and constructed world. Young children will happily work
on the floor so make the most of every surface available, both hard and soft:
tarmac, pavement, grass, sand, bark, walls and fences. The vertical surfaces offered
by fences and walls are an under-used resource in many outdoor spaces and this
dimension is rarely available for children to work on indoors. The big scale
enables the child to work with both hands at the same time, to make big movements that cross the body's midline (which is good for brain development), to
work alongside another child or to make joint creations. When vertical surfaces
are accessible from both sides (such as hanging plastic sheets or Perspex panels),
children can work face to face on this large scale, adding much interaction,

intrigue, experimentation and laughter. Poster paint and chalk will wash off most walls (unless highly porous), but you can also provide surfaces for art work with big boards or pieces of slate. Make boards from marine plywood by painting with emulsion or blackboard paint and coating the back with yacht varnish to reduce warping. Big hooks, such as those made for hanging bikes in a garage, will fit over standard school fences and make the board removable for storage. Painting a permanent base colour onto brick walls with masonry paint will brighten up the space and provide a good surface for children to add temporary artworks with poster paint: permanent murals may look very nice but they can leave little for the children to work with. Cotton sheets, plain shower curtains and rolls of wallpaper lining make great temporary canvases, both laid on the ground and attached to a fence with pegs. The very large vinyl posters that supermarkets and schools advertise with have plain white backs that are perfect for creating a huge, more permanent painting surface – try asking the shop/school or see if parents who work there can help to 'upcycle' those which are no longer wanted.

Boys like to draw, rather than write, and willingly engage in group drawing on the ground with chalks: make sure you have a good supply so that this can develop fully. It is also important to provide small comfortable places where individuals can sit and draw with pencils, crayons and clipboards, having been inspired by something from the world around them: providing several sets of mark-making materials in small transportable tool boxes or writing belts will also support this.

Organising resources for art and mark-making outside

Since art work might take place in many parts of your outdoor space, art materials need to be mobile. They also need to be stored in a way that will keep them well organised and attractively presented as it is very easy for these materials to become muddled so that they inhibit a high-quality creative process. You will need to teach children to look after the resources, replacing them after use, and give attention to keeping resources refreshed and appealing.

Wheeled trolleys with shallow A3 paper trays can be loaded with paper, homemade booklets, previously prepared proformas relating to the role-play theme, mark-making tools, pegs and so on. Shoe organisers from a home-making store provide pockets for mark-making tools such as brushes and kitchen utensils, and some shower curtains also have pockets for bathroom items: these can be tied to a fence near to where children are working. Small plastic tool boxes and caddies made for storing household cleaning items are just right for containing sets of art tools and bottles of paint. These and backpacks are very appealing to children who are exploring schemas of containment and transporting: make sure they are not too heavy. A milk-crate can be a useful container in which to store spray and squirting bottles of ready-mixed paint. Designate shelves in the shed for storing these containers in an accessible way.

Things to work with outside: paint, chalk, drawing and writing

As always, aim to give children experiences that they cannot have indoors and that harness the special nature of being outdoors. It is useful to note that poster paint washes off more easily with a squirt of washing-up liquid. Provide the paint in sturdy pots, trays and bottles. Splash, spray, squirt, drip and print, and use all sorts of application tools and large brushes – a fascinating collection can be made over time from household, garden and decorating suppliers. Use it on big surfaces in a liberated way; experiment on a variety of surfaces; use it thick and use it runny, so that it runs down the painting surface; spray water onto it to see how the colours run, spread and merge; paint on both sides of a large plastic sheet at the same time; paint in the rain and on wet surfaces; hand-print onto walls; squish ready-mix between two layers of clear plastic sheet; put paint into a puddle for children to go through with bikes and wellies; walk along lining paper with bare muddy feet.

Use the stimuli of your surroundings to inspire creative art work, for instance by offering just red and yellow paint in autumn. Tell the inspiring story of Frederick, the mouse who stores up the colours of the summer for the long, cold winter for the other mice: 'and when he told them of the blue periwinkles, the red poppies in the yellow wheat, and the green leaves of the berry bush, they saw the colours as clearly as if they had been painted in their minds' (*Frederick* by Leo Leonni, 1971).

Chalk is an excellent material for use outside, especially as it engages boys in mark-making, and the large spaces available on tarmac, pavement and walls encourage children to work together. They might be inspired to make road layouts of considerable complexity, showing their knowledge of the route to nursery or their own locality. Wet chalk behaves in a different way; suggest chalking onto wet surfaces during or after rain. Chalk easily washes off, which children will be happy to do with water and brushes, or they can observe as the rain gradually removes their marks over time.

There are so many things that inspire children to draw outdoors, especially things from the living world. This is where a well-stocked mobile trolley or tool box is particularly important, so as not to lose the moment. Provide a good range of materials, keep them in good order and observe to find out which best support what children want to do – then improve your provision accordingly. Join children in this activity so that conversation around the drawing enhances the process – group drawing can be particularly powerful at this age.

Likewise, the outdoors can offer many sparks for writing with real purpose and engagement, even for those who do not tend to write indoors. The adult role includes being alert and prepared to capture and fan these sparks. Signs, notices and labels are often needed, especially for role play and the growing area; play might require a treasure map, instructions or secret messages; children might want to record birds and insects they've seen or to compile a *Book of Questions and Ideas*.

Things to work with outside: natural materials, elements from the weather and new perspectives

Natural materials lend themselves to creative use, both temporary and permanent: they have intrinsic beauty and can be endlessly manipulated to make patterns, mosaics, pictures, sculptures and shapes on the ground. Add coloured and sparkly items, such as glass beads, to increase the visual and tactile appeal. Large cobbles painted with bright colours and then varnished make lovely resources for pattern-making. Shells and pebbles embedded into plaster, clay or cement can make stepping stones to place amongst plants or across grass.

Use mud, very wet sand, gloop (cornflower with water and food colouring) and slime (soap flakes whisked with water) or shaving foam to sculpt, drip and make marks with sticks and fingers. Use the many opportunities that the weather provides for creative play and mark-making, such as making prints, tracks and patterns in snow with feet, twigs or a broom, 'snow angels' by lying on the ground and models of snow people and animals. Helen Bromley provides a great list of mark-making possibilities from rain, fog, frost, snow, wind and sun in her book *Making My Own Mark* (2006, pp. 57–58) and recommends that a laminated copy is kept to hand with a 'weather box'. Shadows are a particularly intriguing phenomenon for creative explorations on bright days in both summer and winter. For example, children might make shadow shapes with their body, hands and objects on the ground, on walls or on a white sheet hung between trees; chalk around shadow shapes; and explore shadow effects such as dappled light under a tree with a camera.

Creativity is also inspired when children are offered new ways of looking at the world. Try looking close up with magnifiers and homemade viewers made from a kitchen paper roll or a square cut out of a cardboard frame; being shrunk to the size of an ant with special spectacles; being up high and far away with telescope or binoculars; or seeing upside down while hanging from a cross-bar. Explore the world through large sheets of coloured acetate, looking also at the coloured shadows it creates. Cameras are an excellent way to refocus on familiar things and remember too that children already look at the world in a very different way to adults: listen carefully to what they have to say.

Providing for weaving and sculpture outdoors

Resources for weaving, sculpture and woodwork outdoors

Garden mesh and netting
Garden trellis and willow panels
Bread and milk crates
Orange plastic builder's mesh (Harris netting)
Oven trays
Willow and bamboo garden canes (tape the ends to protect eyes)

Floristry ribbon, silk ribbons, crepe paper
Wool, string, rope, upholstery tape
A good range of 1 m lengths of colourful and shiny fabrics
Colourful plastic supermarket carrier bags (cut into strips)
Tinsel and Christmas garlands
Old CDs, beads, bottle tops, shells and other shiny or attractive items
Natural materials
Plastic door screens (from shops such as *Evolution*)
A very long rope (old climber's ropes are ideal)
Cardboard boxes, carpet roll tubes, plastic reels
Logs, tree trunk slices, branch segments, twigs
Soft wood off-cuts

If you have wire-mesh fences around your outdoor space, you have plenty of ready-made canvas for weaving on a grand scale. Young children are often fascinated by the schematic concepts of 'in and out', 'going through' and 'connecting' and this is also a great way to improve the look of your boundaries, especially where the view beyond is unattractive or your outdoor space is too open. Weaving is a good activity for the muscle development needed for writing as well as a satisfying expressive experience. Although some weaving will remain as permanent works of art, there should also be lots of opportunity for temporary weaving with a range of fine and coarse meshes for increasing dexterity: fences around the boundaries, wooden trellis and willow panels, plastic meshes and netting from garden centres. The orange plastic temporary fencing used at building sites (Harris netting) is just the right size for small hands, which is easier than weaving into smaller spaces with the fingers. Trellis and willow panels can be worked on from both sides, making ideal partitions to delineate a quiet zone in the outdoor space. For very small outdoor spaces, an oven tray attached to a brick wall sticks out enough for children to weave with strips of fabric, ribbon and crepe paper. Children interested in this kind of activity will find other places for weaving and tying knots, such as the grid on the base of milk and bread crates and the branches of small trees. On a larger scale, garden canes pushed into grass makes a very coarse weave: if the canes are positioned well apart, children will be able to go in and out themselves as they weave with long ropes, giving an experience they can feel with their whole body (the song *In and Out the Dusty Bluebells* would go well with this movement). A maypole made by setting a broom handle into a bucket of cement and attaching several lengths of colourful floristry ribbon, combines dance with a weaving action. Aim to replace or extend permanent weaving annually, so that new children have taken part; a family weaving day is an excellent way to get unsightly fences covered up.

Collect lots of materials for weaving and store in tubs or trugs from which children can make their selections: rope, colourful string, tinsel, spun and un-spun wool, strips of fabric, colourful supermarket carrier bags, florist and silk ribbons, bendy twigs and anything else that can be woven at this scale. Also collect colourful, shiny and natural items that can be threaded or tied into the weaving: old CDs, shells, small plastic toys, beads, buttons, leaves and so on.

Decorating things around the outdoor area will also prove very popular. Providing a good selection of tinsel strands in buckets will transform your outdoor area around Christmas time. Decorate a tree with anything that comes to mind by tying things onto branches and twig ends. The strands from ornate plastic door screens (used to deter flies from entering in the summer) are visually pleasing when tied in branches, moving in the wind and making a labyrinth-like area for children to move amongst. Homemade windsocks and banners can be made by tie-dying cotton fabric with cold-water dye. Children might also use the fabrics provided for imaginative play to make 'Art Attack' style 'paintings' on the grass.

With the space available outdoors, there is plenty of scope for sculpture on a big scale too. Willow and bamboo canes, cardboard boxes, cardboard tubes from carpet rolls, plastic reels, wood and other found, natural and recycled materials make excellent resources. Children might use cardboard boxes and fabric pieces to make dragon monsters which they can then wear for a dance procession, much like a Chinese Dragon, accompanied by large and noisy homemade musical instruments.

Providing for music and dance outdoors

Resources for music outdoors

Big plastic and metal containers and buckets
Old metal dustbins or other very large containers
Metal, wooden and plastic spoons and brushes
Lengths of plastic and copper piping in a range of diameters and lengths (from DIY stores)
Plastic funnels, cardboard tubes for megaphones
Tins and pots for shakers
Old saucepans and lids (school kitchen equipment is ideal)
Old cutlery
Natural materials, sticks
Washing lines
Wind-chimes
Large and robust percussion instruments from around the world
World music on CD, portable player
Bread crates, stepping stones

Figure 5.3 Musicality can be incorporated into every part of the outdoor space.

Young children need to experience music every day and there is nowhere better than the outdoors for this, where they are liberated to make a high-energy, noisy response and where there is stimulation from the environment itself to make sounds and be musical with their whole body. Musical behaviour can occur anywhere in the outdoor space, so be sure not to confine it to a particular place. However, you might construct some music-making structures in appropriate spots – bear in mind how noisy they are likely to be! The best approach is to consider how 'musicality' can be incorporated into every part of your space and into as many activities as possible, with singing, dancing and rhythmical move-ment being an integral part of all play outdoors. Make use of the equipment and resources you already have, such as hopping along stepping stones in time to a chant or bouncing along a row of upturned bread crates in a movement sequence. Encourage children to explore their own voice through these too, perhaps by making increasingly higher-pitched noises as they go up the steps of the slide, shouting from the top and making a descending 'wheeee' sound as they slide down. Sticks and wooden or metal spoons can be scraped along the textured surfaces of walls, railings and fences, and the voice can be amplified down plastic pipes with funnels at each end or along guttering pipes. Children might explore the sounds they can make by sending objects down plastic guttering tubes and hit the ends with a spongy table tennis bat or flip-flop – different lengths and diameters will produce differently pitched sounds. This could progress into making a giant rain-stick with gravel inside by covering both ends of the pipe with pieces of cloth held with large elastic bands.

Simple but effective outdoor instruments are easy to make, and these can be much more effective at harnessing the special nature of the outdoors than simply bringing indoor instruments outdoors! Once given the idea, children might make lots of different shakers by putting natural materials inside a range of containers, such as a biscuit tin or flower pot. Encourage them to find out how big and noisy the shakers can be. Collect a few big plastic and metal containers, such as a dustbin or compost bin and upturned buckets, and supply big spoons, brushes and other household utensils for drumming. Try this under a gazebo canopy in heavy rain for a really amazing effect and play African drumming music to the children afterwards (the *Stomp Out Loud* DVD has a remarkable sequence of drumming in the rain too – see resources at the end of this chapter). Such large containers with lids can also be rolled around with stones or cobbles inside to make thrillingly noisy and vibrant sounds. Old pans and lids, the bigger the better, can be hung along a washing line with spoons as strikers – painting them with oil-based paint will increase durability outside and make them attractive (metal will require a layer of undercoat first). Try making wind-chimes from old cutlery, shells and dried clay pieces to add to those bought from shops. Use the *Stomp Out Loud* and *Stomp: Rhythms of the World* DVDs to spark innovative ideas with the children: the musician/dancers use an amazing range of everyday items, such as brooms, drainpipes and buckets, to make fantastic, energetic musical rhythms.

In the suggestions made so far, very little money has been needed to make a creative musical environment, but you can augment your provision for music outdoors with a selection of robust world percussion instruments, to be used with vigour, action and plenty of movement. There are lots of suitable types of music too, from lively jigs, flamenco, South American, African, carnival and classical for inspiring a direct response, to mood music for creating an atmosphere for pretend play, such as sounds of the jungle. Collect nursery rhymes for marching and dancing, and songs that you all like to sing, changing the words to fit whatever it is that the children are doing, such as, 'This is the way we slide down the slide....' Laminate lists so that you are never short of ideas and singing becomes a part of everyday outdoor play. A portable CD player or ICT device enables children to listen to music and rhymes in a quiet area outdoors and to record their own voices, performances or sounds around the outdoor environment. Settings that are newly built or refurbished should have an electrical supply installed in their outdoor space.

Resources for dance outdoors

Ribbons, ribbon sticks, bubbles and balloons
Feathers and leaves
Attractive scarves, pieces of voile fabric
Soft pony-tail bands
Homemade maypole
Wrist and ankle bells
Maracas, castanets, hand drums
World music on CD, portable player (see Chapter 4 for suggestions)

Music and dance go together especially strongly for young children, who experience feelings and ideas with their whole body. Be ready to capture the creative sparks that are ignited by being outside. Children might be spontaneously inspired to twirl and dance simply by chasing falling leaves on a windy day, by responding to the movements of their shadow on a sunny day or by jumping to catch sparkling bubbles on a bright spring day. They might make animal movements, such as bunnies hopping, horses galloping and lions charging. Encourage children to explore highly active movements and to come up with appropriate names for them: children's words might well be more interesting than the 'correct' one, although you can also use this as a playful way to increase their vocabulary (see the section on movement language in Chapter 4). Use exotic words and alliteration, such as slip, slide and slither, as many children of four and above love to play with the sounds of words.

Figure 5.4 Young children need very little stimulus to spontaneously twirl and dance!

Ensure that your instrument collection includes those that encourage movement and dance, such as wrist and ankle bells, maracas and hand drums, and encourage the exploration of movements to make sounds. Select music from all over the world and a range of genres for its potential to inspire children to run, twirl and leap: *William Tell*, *Carmen* and *The Flight of the Bumblebee* are particularly good for this, as is carnival music. There are many types of world music that are excellent for dance outdoors – explore them with the children and make your own special collection of the ones that work best. A carnival procession brings together music and dance, perhaps with banners you have made previously. Provide props such as pieces of beautiful and floaty fabric, ribbon sticks and bubbles. Ribbons and lightweight scarves can be tied to pony-tail bands so that children can wear them on their wrists. This is particularly helpful for balloons, to prevent them floating away. Remember that some children are frightened by bursting balloons and that the pieces of rubber can present a choking hazard for children and wildlife.

Providing for imaginative play, stories and performance outdoors

Resources for imaginative play outdoors

Blankets, sheets, old curtains and net curtains
Pegs, string, rope, pulleys
Pop-up tent, clothes horse
Construction materials (see Chapter 6 for suggestions)
Pieces of fabric in a range of sizes: large; cape-sized; scarf-sized strips for turbans and belts
A variety of types of fabric to spark different themes, e.g. camouflage, white, shiny, blue
Hats, bags, baskets
Soft toys, puppets, dolls
Torches, telephones
Natural materials
Carpet squares, small rug
Bikes, carts, transporters
Short lengths of plastic piping (for fire-fighting or making speaking tubes)
Cardboard boxes: big and small, cardboard carpet-roll tubes, etc.
Trolley(s) with mark-making resources, joining materials, creative materials, small-world resources
Specific items to support a particular role-play theme
Themed sets of small-world resources in suitable containers
Materials for small-world landscapes, such as flower pots, logs and big stones
Aggregates for small-world landscapes
Containers for small-world landscape materials, such as tyres and planters

I am enough of an artist to draw freely upon my imagination. Imagination is more important than knowledge. Knowledge is limited. Imagination encircles the world.

(Albert Einstein)

Imaginative play outdoors

Children between three and seven engage in a great deal of imaginative play, starting with imitative pretend play that draws directly on known experiences and developing into complex fantasy play in which scene and story are negotiated by several children playing together, and which takes place in an imaginative space shared between them. Imaginative play is therefore an important ingredient for rich and satisfying outdoor play provision. This is not difficult because the outdoors is rich in potential for supplying stimulation, contexts and materials for imaginative play of all types. Because of the role of imaginative play in processing real experiences, themes for imaginative play should for the most part come from children's own interests: our task is to know what children want to do and to make an environment that is filled with possibilities to match this. Young children have many of their own themes for imaginative play and, like traditional nursery stories, these derive from the deep concerns and preoccupations of the younger members of a highly social species: universal themes are belonging, families and friendship; good, bad and power; threats, danger, getting lost and being found. Respond to what you notice has interest or relevance, both through observations and from conversations with parents, and ensure that the play you provide for relates to the cultural contexts of the children in your setting. As an example, while football is an imaginative play activity for many young boys, especially during the World Cup, cricket may be more significant for boys in Asian families.

By setting up outdoor provision with an emphasis on spontaneous imaginative play, we lay the ground for children to use their own imaginations and creativity. There is, of course, a place for planned and pre-constructed themes outdoors, but do involve children in making the decisions, in collecting the materials and in creating the site – they are likely to get far more from this approach than being offered a ready-made play scene. Children can become passive players, expecting a scenario to be provided and so losing a big part of their own imaginative drive and creative abilities; this has already happened in many parts of modern children's lives. The most effective provision offers resources and places as part of what is continuously available so that, as ideas are sparked, they can be played out straight away.

Because of the very long list of possible themes for imaginative play outside, it is important that permanent play structures are not too defined. Do not make the mistake of installing an overly preconceived structure: a simple wooden house or a basic structure that can be modified and embellished has the most potential and will remain of interest and value for longer. A small wooden shed can become whatever you want and can easily be changed for a new theme – discuss and decide with the children what kind of place it should be for the current season, and involve them in fitting it out appropriately. Some settings have a real rowing

Figure 5.5 Sticks on the barbecue re-enact the real sausages cooking on the nearby campfire.

boat, donated after it is no longer water-worthy, and these too have a lot of play potential – there is something about the space inside a boat that works well for children's imaginations. Supplement this with temporary structures and lots of resources that children can add to the basic structure to create a site with lots of imaginative play value. Even young children are quite able to use their imaginations to transform and, as discussed in Chapter 2, representation is something we want them to do. It is quite likely that some of the limited ability of today's children to play imaginatively, which early years practitioners often remark upon, is due to over-use of preconceived play equipment and toys.

An outdoor space that has plenty of small nooks and crannies where children can feel out of sight or secret, and several different ground surfaces and heights, will offer much stimulus for imagination; children especially love to be underneath and up high. Plants that children can play amongst, such as grasses, bamboo and willow, give an atmosphere of exotic lands, even if this area is quite small.

Provide den-building resources so that children make the child-sized and private spaces from which pretend and fantasy play so often develop. Dens can be used for home play, camping, being an adventurer or explorer, and even as a bear cave (see Chapter 6).

The best props for imaginative play of all types are flexible and open-ended: children can use them to take on many roles and this also means you need to provide less. Fabric, in a range of colours, textures and sizes, is an excellent prop from which children can make shelters, capes, robes, headdresses and belts. Fabric is also very good at suggesting a theme for the imagination to work on. Select fabrics on the basis of how versatile they are: a large piece of blue could be the sea, a river, a lake or the sky; white might be snow or clouds, something shiny could be treasure, a king's robe, fairy wings or a magician's cloak; camouflage material could be the earth, a cave or the jungle. With a good range of fabric pieces, dressing-up clothes are not really needed, with the exception perhaps of safety jackets and mechanic's overalls. Do, however, collect hats, bags and baskets, and encourage children to bring out soft toys and puppets from indoors when the weather is suitable. Anything made from fabric is best stored indoors, especially through the winter, so organise them in easy-to-move containers. A wicker trunk, a suitcase and a shopping trolley are all ideal and can often become part of the play themselves. Lightweight laundry baskets and plastic tubs with handles also work well for storage and easy access.

Some planned themes for role play are more suited to the outdoor environment or will extend indoor themes, and there is actually a long list of exciting and meaningful possibilities:

- Home play, camping, picnic, barbecue, beach, holiday, lighthouse keeper...
- Garage/mechanic/MOT, car wash, truck/digger, construction site, train engineers...
- Police, fire-fighting, ambulance, road-crossing, painter, window-cleaning, washday...
- Pirates, treasure hunting, boat, castle, fairies, magic carpet, witches/magicians, cave, island, explorer, archaeologist...

Figure 5.6 With fabric, children can make shelters, capes, robes, head dresses and belts.

- Traditional nursery stories, especially those that take place in a forest...
- Café, drive-through, supermarket, garden centre, market stall, vets, farm...
- Post and parcel delivery service, removals, Father Christmas, train station, airport runway...

If a theme has been particularly successful, keep a list of the additional resources you used, for easy gathering next time this theme comes up. Bike play is well suited to many of these themes so do take the opportunities that arise to extend and enrich children's use of vehicles. Include literacy wherever it makes sense and has meaning, such as booking in for your vehicle's MOT or a police officer recording the number plate of a bike that has transgressed the rules! Give vehicles numbered parking spaces and use carts and baskets to deliver addressed letters and parcels; in December, you could have a present-wrapping station indoors and a loading bay outside for a cart transformed into a sleigh. Letters written indoors can also be delivered to posting boxes around the outdoor area with a special post bag.

Another way to support imaginative use of the outdoor area is to make signs, such as supermarket logos, café menus and order pads, delivery times on the post boxes, number plates on bikes, house numbers and notices such as 'danger: men at work', 'buy petrol here', 'smell me' and 'this way to the magic dell'. Children might also arrive in the morning to find a 'help me' letter with a problem that needs solving or a treasure map to follow. When children are used to including writing and drawing in their imaginative play, they will want to do their own, so keep a trolley of suitable materials well stocked.

Figure 5.7 There is huge potential for small-world play outside that captures the special nature of the outdoors.

There is also huge potential for small-world imaginative play outside with many little landscapes available everywhere, in sand and soil, in grass and amongst plants, and in puddles and cracks in pavement and tarmac. Encourage children to use flower pots, logs and stones to make homes, hills and roads. If your space is limited to tarmac, you can also create some extra landscapes by filling tyres or planters with various interesting aggregates, such as white chippings for an arctic landscape or sandstone pebbles for a desert. Grass grown in a soil-filled tyre offers long-grass jungles and short-grass prairies; children will enjoy cutting long grass back with scissors! Keep themed sets of small-world resources in containers that children can easily carry to the place they have chosen to play: dinosaurs, British wildlife, wild animals, arctic animals, domestic and farm animals, mini-beasts, vehicles, play people, fairies and so on. It is better to have a central storage trolley from which children can select than to place sets yourself, as children may well come up with more inventive combinations and ideas. Make sure that plentiful supplies of natural materials are also to hand for this play.

Stories, books and story-telling outdoors

Resources for stories, books and story-telling outdoors

Collections of books and rhymes related to the main aspects of provision outdoors
Collections of books and poems that read well outside
Collections of books and poems that are good starting points for further activity
Collections of books, poems and rhymes that support predictable interests from
    being outside
Audio books and portable player(s)
Baskets and other containers for small selections that can be carried by children
Picnic rugs, cushions, carpet squares
Tent, parasol, large umbrella, hammock

Stories, books and story-telling outdoors

For most young children between three and seven, stories make more sense than the real world. Putting something in terms of a narrative seems to help them to both understand and to put their own ideas into words: this is why we deal with complex issues such as feelings and guidelines for behaviour with puppets, books and tales. It also shows in children's love of books and story-telling, both of which should be provided for outside just as much as inside. For some children, having a story read outside, rather than indoors, makes them more likely to participate. Some stories are perfect for telling and exploring outside; the setting may reflect the context of the story and being outside creates an atmosphere for listening to it and a place for re-enacting it.

Books make excellent starting points for much further activity, especially imaginative play (see the lists of children's books in each chapter). In *Exercising Muscles and Minds* (2003, pp. 67–69), Marjorie Ouvry sets out an extensive array of possible lines of development in every area of learning from *Mrs Mopple's Washing Line* (Anita Hewitt, 1994). In *Making My Own Mark* (2006, pp. 55–57), literacy expert Helen Bromley gives an analysis of possible learning outdoors for language, reading and writing that could be built into long-term plans, starting from the book *Where's Julius?* (John Burningham, 2001).

Your outdoor area needs lots of good places for looking at and sharing books, for telling stories, acting them out and adapting them, and for composing your own stories together. Books are most effective outside with very small groups, perhaps just one or two children with an adult, so you can choose the spot depending on the book. The most important conditions are comfort and atmosphere, such as near or amongst plants for a jungle feel. Ideal places to share stories and conversation are in a swing seat or hammock, under an arbour or pergola, on a picnic blanket or magic carpet, under a big umbrella in the rain or a parasol in the sun. To create a book area, provide small collections in a basket or caddie with a blanket and cushions or inside a tent or den. A large tractor tyre also makes an excellent story-telling circle that can also be used for discussions, review and eating a snack together.

Throughout this book, I have listed children's books and rhymes for supporting the main aspects of provision outdoors, because we know that children are strongly engaged by these themes. Books and poems for outdoors should also be selected because they are especially good for reading outside, because of the

Figure 5.8 Being together and chatting is a great way to begin a new story.

atmosphere in this environment or because we can capitalise on the greater freedom for an active response (such as the classic *We're Going on a Bear Hunt* by Michael Rosen and Helen Oxenbury, 2001); because they make good starting points for imaginative and creative play outdoors (such as *Frederick* by Leo Lionni, 1971); and because they support predictable interests arising from being outdoors, such as mini-beasts, wind, snow, vehicles, friendship and superheroes. Helen Bromley lists her ten top books for inspiring writing through play outdoors in *Making My Own Mark* (2006, p. 54) and these are included in the suggested books below with kind permission (marked with ^). Do not forget to include audio books with a portable player so that children can take one to their preferred spot to listen, submerging themselves in the story's atmosphere.

Performance and drama outdoors

Resources for performance and drama outdoors

Puppets, soft toys, dolls
A pair of old curtains
Hats, bags, jewellery
Instruments, microphone or karaoke machine
Bread crates, wooden pallet, carpet tiles
Mark-making materials for making tickets, advertisements and signage

Story-telling, play with puppets, singing and dancing can all extend into a performance for those children who enjoy having an audience, especially for the older children in this age range (for the younger children, they are more likely to be fairly spontaneous and short). A simple stage can be made from up-turned bread-crates (best tied or Velcro-strapped together for stability), or a wooden pallet is just the right size for a larger and more permanent one. Curtains hung from tree branches make a good puppet theatre, or you can mark out a screen with chalk on a wall for a shadow performance. Role-play props will provide fabric, hats, bags and jewellery for dressing up and a microphone will inspire imitation of modern singers, especially Pop Idol and X Factor type scenarios. Seating can be made from milk crates and carpet tiles will make them more comfortable! Position mark-making materials nearby, in case posters or tickets are wanted.

Making the most of creative and imaginative play

A camera is a really useful resource for this aspect of provision, especially as many creative 'products' outdoors are ephemeral, communal and cannot be kept or taken home. Recording the *process* of creation allows you to examine children's involvement and plan next steps with other staff, to share and value it with parents and to review the experience and stimulate new ideas with children.

Children love to see themselves in images and can become quite skilled with a camera themselves. Progress to a digital camera as soon as you feel they can use it properly as this opens up the art of photography itself and in particular gives children a way of conveying their perspectives and values in a way that their language cannot yet express. Robust digital cameras and video cameras are now available at reasonable cost from educational suppliers.

The need for children to have an abundance of unstructured and uninterrupted time cannot be over-emphasised. Good-quality creative and imaginative play sessions will not develop if time outdoors is short and children do not know whether they will be able to go outside the next day. They must know that they will have access to long periods outdoors every day for their interests to develop and involvement to become deep. Opportunity for repetition, trial-and-error and reflection gives time for ideas to emerge and for mastery of new skills; they also build the dispositions needed for creative endeavour and problem-solving, such as concentration and persistence. Children may well want to return to a project later in the day or the next day, so the question for us is: how can we leave some projects outside so that children can continue to develop them?

The adult role is very sensitive in supporting imaginative play. Young children love to have an adult's involvement but they will often let you take over the direction of play, which is all too easy to do! An attentive adult who waits before they act, while seeking to understand what is going on in the children's minds will be able to make small suggestions or simply offer further resources to support and continue the play. Look for natural ways of simply being together and letting conversation flow, in and out of other activities – the 'back-burner' thinking of intuitive, subconscious brain processes is just as important as more directed, logical reasoning. There can be a need for young children to be taught new skills or ideas so that they can expand their own repertoire for future use. If the role-play theme is not very familiar, the adult will need to model role behaviour, language and play ideas to make it a success for the children (Wingate Nursery's *Outdoor Banking* DVD is an excellent example of this). However, the best role play derives from something the child knows a lot about and has plenty of personal experience to work with – in this the adult can take a more 'supporting' role, responding rather than leading. Above all, it is important to value children's creative and imaginative play outdoors highly, using observation opportunities to find out what is in or on a child's mind, as well as what he or she can do for formative and summative assessments. It is in this play that you are likely to see the true extent of the child's knowledge, interests, capacities and dispositions.

It is important to consider the needs of every individual in making provision for this area, and how they might interact with each other. Older children are the very best tutors for younger children's play, and this is particularly so with imaginative play. Consider how you can have mixed ages in outdoor play, as so much is lost by having separate play sessions. Evaluate your provision frequently to ensure that experiences relate to all cultures within the setting and be alert to stereotyping. Gender differences can be very noticeable in imaginative play outside, where boys tend to be much more boisterous than girls: how much do we value what is actually happening in rough-and-tumble or superhero play, and are girls' needs fully met outside?

> *The creation of something new is not accomplished by the intellect alone but by the play instinct. The creative mind plays with the object it loves.*
>
> (C.J. Jung)

> *The only way to prepare for spontaneity is to have well stocked cupboards.*
>
> (Teacher Tom blog post, 13 August 2010)

Children's books to support painting and mark-making

★A Journey into the World of Fantasy with Hundertwasser (Painting Book) Prestel (Prestel Publishing 2008)

Angel Pavement Quentin Blake (Red Fox 2005)

Bear Hunt Anthony Browne (Puffin Books 2010)

Bear's Magic Pencil Anthony Browne (HarperCollins Children's Books 2010)

Chidi Only Likes Blue: An African book of colours Ifeoma Onyefulu (Frances Lincoln Children's Books 1997)

Colours in Nature: Blue Barbara Hunter (Heinemann Library 2003)

Colours in Nature: Green Barbara Hunter (Heinemann Library 2003)

Colours in Nature: Red Barbara Hunter (Heinemann Library 2003)

Colours in Nature: Yellow Lisa Bruce (Heinemann Library 2003)

Draw Me a Star Eric Carle (Puffin Books 1995)

Follow the Line Simone Lia (Mammoth 2002)

Frederick Leo Lionni (Hodder and Stoughton 1971)

★Grandfather's Pencil and the Room of Stories Michael Foreman (Red Fox 1995)

Gregory and the Magic Line Dawn Piggott (Orion Children's 2003)

Hands: Growing up to be an artist Lois Ehlert (Harcourt Children's Books 2004)

Harold and the Purple Crayon Crockett Johnson (HarperCollins Children's Books 1992)

Harold's Fairy Tale: Further adventures with the purple crayon Crockett Johnson (HarperCollins Australia 1994)

★Ish Peter H. Reynolds (Walker Books 2005)

Lines That Wiggle Candace Whitman and Steve Wilson (Blue Apple Books 2007)

Little Blue and Little Yellow Leo Lionni (William Morrow 1996)

Matthew's Dream Leo Lionni (Dragonfly Books 1995)

Mister Seahorse Eric Carle (Puffin Books 2006)

My Many Coloured Days Dr Seuss, Steve Johnson and Lou Fancher (Red Fox 2001)

Planting a Rainbow Lois Ehlert (Voyager Books 1992)

The Dot Peter H. Reynolds (Walker Books 2004)

The Feather Dot Cleeve and Kim Harley (Tamarind 2003)

★The Magic Paintbrush Julia Donaldson and Joel Stewart (Macmillan Children's Books 2004)

★The Pencil Allan Ahlberg and Bruce Ingman (Walker Books 2009)

★The Shape Game Anthony Browne (Corgi Children's Books 2004)

The Squiggle Carole Lexa Schaefer and Pierr Morgan (Random House Children's Books 2000)
★*Wabi Sabi* Mark Reibstein and Ed Young (Little, Brown & Company 2008)
Winnie the Witch Valerie Thomas and Korky Paul (OUP Oxford 2006)

Children's books to support dancing and music-making

★*A Very Proper Fox* Jan Fearnley (HarperCollins Children's Books 2006)
Bumpus Jumpus Dinosaurumpus! Tony Mitton and Guy Parker-Rees (Orchard Books 2003)
Doing the Animal Bop Jan Ormerod and Lindsey Gardiner (OUP Oxford 2005)
Down by the Cool of the Pool Tony Mitton and Guy Parker-Rees (Orchard Books 2002)
Farmer Joe and the Music Show Tony Mitton and Guy Parker-Rees (Orchard Books 2009)
Giraffes Can't Dance Giles Andreae and Guy Parker-Rees (Orchard Books 2001)
Noisy Parade: A Hullabaloo Safari Jakki Wood (Francis Lincoln 2002)
Rumble in the Jungle (book and CD) Giles Andreae and David Wojtowycz (Orchard Books 2006)
Saturday Night at the Dinosaur Stomp Carol Diggory Shields and Scott Nash (Walker Books 2008)
Spookyrumpus Tony Mitton and Guy Parker-Rees (Orchard Books 2005)
Sunny Robin Mitchell and Judith Steedman (Simply Read Books 2003)
The Animal Boogie: A Barefoot singalong Debbie Harter (Barefoot Books 2011)
The Dance of the Dinosaurs Colin and Jacqui Hawkins (HarperCollins Children's Books 2002)
The Dancing Tiger Malachy Doyle, Steve Johnson and Lou Fancher (Simon & Schuster 2005)
★*The Frog Ballet* Amanda McCardie (Red Fox 1997)

Children's books to support imaginative play

An Island in the Sun Stella Blackstone and Nicoletta Ceccoli (Barefoot Books 2003)
^*Blue Rabbit and the Runaway Wheel* Chris Wormwell (Red Fox 2001)
Dear Zoo Rod Campbell (Campbell Books 2001)
Free Fall David Wiesner (Willliam Morrow 1991)
Going Shopping Sarah Garland (Frances Lincoln Children's Books 2008)
Goldilocks and the Three Bears Barbara Mitchelhill and Michelle Mathers (Collins Educational 2005)
Greedy Zebra Mwenye Hadithi and Adrienne Kennaway (Hodder Children's Books 1984)
Hansel and Gretel Anthony Browne (Walker Books 2008)
^*Harry and the Dinosaurs Romp in the Swamp* Ian Whybrow and Adrian Reynolds (Puffin Books 2009)
If . . . Sarah Perry (J. Paul Getty Museum 1995)
If We Had a Sailboat Jonathan Emmett and Adrian Reynolds (Oxford University Press 2006)
★*Imagine a Day* Sarah L. Thomson and Rob Gonsalves (Atheneum Books 2005)
★*Imagine a Night* Sarah L. Thomson and Rob Gonsalves (Atheneum Books 2000)
★*Imagine a Place* Sarah L. Thomson and Rob Gonsalves (Atheneum Books 2008)

Jack and the Beanstalk Richard Walker and Niamh Sharkey (Barefoot Books 2006)

Little Red Riding Hood Katherine McEwan (Collins Educational 2010)

My Cat Likes to Hide in Boxes Eve Sutton and Lynley Dodd (Puffin Books 1978)

Mr Gumpy's Motor Car John Burningham (Red Fox 2002)

^*Mr Gumpy's Outing* John Burningham (Red Fox 2001)

My Mother's Sari Sandhya Rao and Nina Sabnani (North-South Books 2009)

Please Don't Chat to the Bus Driver Shen Roddie and Jill Newton (Bloomsbury Publishing 2001)

Port Side Pirates Oscar Seaworthy and Debbie Carter (Barefoot Books 2011)

Shadow Suzy Lee (Chronicle Books 2010)

^*Someone Bigger* Jonathan Emmett and Adrian Reynolds (Oxford University Press 2003)

Starlight Sailor James Mayhew and Jackie Morris (Barefoot Books 2009)

The Dancing Dragon Marcia Vaughan and Stanley W. Foon (Mondo Publishing 1996)

^*The Green Ship* Quentin Blake (Red Fox 2000)

The Gruffalo Julia Donaldson and Axel Scheffler (Macmillan Children's Books 1999)

The Jolly Postman Allan Ahlberg and Janet Ahlberg (Puffin Books 1999)

★*The Once Upon a Time Map Book* B.G. Hennessy and Peter Joyce (Candlewick Press 2010)

The Shopping Basket John Burningham (Red Fox 1992)

The Shopping Expedition Allan Ahlberg and Andre Amstutz (Walker Books 2006)

The Swirling Hijaab Na'ima bint Robert and Nilesh Mistry (Mantra Lingua 2002)

^*The Train Ride* June Crebbin and Stephen Lambert (Walker Books 1996)

The Treasure Hunt (Tales from Percy's Park) Nick Butterworth (HarperCollins Children's Books 2011)

Tim, Ted and the Pirates Ian Whybrow and Russell Ayto (HarperCollins Children's Books 2013)

^*Treasure Hunt* Allan Ahlberg and Gillian Tyler (Walker Books 2003)

^*Walking Through the Jungle* Julie Lacome (Walker Books 1995)

^*We're Going on a Bear Hunt* Michael Rosen and Helen Oxenbury (Walker Books 2009)

Whatever Next! Jill Murphy (Macmillan Children's Books 2007)

^*Where's Julius?* John Burningham (Red Fox 2001)

Further information and resources – source material

Andy Goldsworthy: A collaboration with nature Andy Goldsworthy (Harry N. Abrams Inc. 1998) – Andy Goldsworthy is an artist who works with natural materials in the landscape in a most remarkable way: fabulous colour photographs

A Whole World Katy Couprie and Antonin Louchard (Milet Publishing 2002)

Calendars and postcards with colour, art and photography themes: there are many high-quality images available in card and book shops, such as the *Nouvelles Images* range, www.nouvellesimages.com

Colourful World Amandine Guisez Gallienne and Hilton McConnico (Thames & Hudson 2005)

Hundertwasser Calendar 2013 Benedikt Taschen (Taschen 2012) – use individual images for direct stimulus or display

Hundertwasser Kunst Haus Wein (Album) Joham Harel and Wieland Schmied (Taschen 1999) – both painting and buildings by this artist/architect offer great stimulation for imaginative responses

Natural: Simple land art through the seasons – a really inspirational and visual book filled with colour images (with very little text) of work by nature artist Marc Poyet – many are similar to what young children might do (Francis Lincoln 2009)

Parkland Andy Goldsworthy (Yorkshire Sculpture Park 1988) – lovely collection of ephemeral works of art with natural materials through the seasons

Prints of works of art with outdoor relevance: calendars are a great source (individual prints can be laminated for use outside); high-street art shops, such as Athena, have quite cheap prints (keep the plastic film on for outdoor use); download prints from Internet art sites. There are very many possible works; here are some examples:

- *Landscapes*, such as Wolf Kahn, Paul Powis (*Seeing a whisper*), Giuliana Lazzerini (*Village at sunset*), Vincent Van Gogh (*Wheatfield with cypresses*), John Miller (*Moon over the bay*), H. Leung (*Mountain glory*);
- *Colour*, such as Jackson Pollack, Wassily Kandinsky (*Farbstudie Quadrate*), Gustav Klimt (*Pear tree*), Laffanki (*Silent valley*), Nel Whatmore (*Colour field 3*);
- *Children playing outside*, such as L.S. Lowry (*On the sands*), Pieter Bruegel (*Children's games*);
- *Mosaics*, such as the works of Antoni Gaudi.

The Elements of Design: Rediscovering colours, textures, forms and shapes Loan Oei and Cecile De Kegel (Thames & Hudson 2002) – wonderful source book of colour photographs of pattern and form in the environment

The Five Senses Herve Tullet (Tate Publishing 2004)

Wabi Sabi: The art of everyday life Diane Durston (Storey Books 2006) – collection of sayings around the theme of beauty in the simple and ordinary

www.artnet.com – information on artists and art movements

www.artgroup.com – for online mail order prints, including prints from the Tate

www.allposters.co.uk – for online mail order posters, including landscapes and fine art

Further information and resources – art and mark-making

Children, Art, Artists: The expressive languages of children, the artistic language of Alberto Burri Reggio Children (Reggio Children 2004) – has a fabulous section on children's use of natural materials, available from Sightlines Initiative's online store, www.sightlines-initiative.com

Everything Has A Shadow, Except Ants (Reggio Children 1999), available from Sightlines Initiative's online store, www.sightlines-initiative.com

It's Not a Bird Yet: The drama of drawing Ursula Kolbe (Peppinot Press 2005) – super description of the process of drawing by young children, especially the power of group drawing, available from Sightlines Initiative's online store, www.sightlines-initiative.com

Making My Own Mark: Play and writing Helen Bromley (British Association for Early Childhood Education 2006)

Nature's Playground Fiona Danks and Jo Schofield (Frances Lincoln 2006) – includes many inspiring possible creative opportunities

Rapunzel's Supermarket: About young children and their art Ursula Kolbe (2nd edition, Peppinot Press 2007), available from Sightlines Initiative's online store, www.sightlines-initiative.com

The Little Book of Mark Making Elaine Massey and Sam Goodman (Featherstone Education 2007)

The Little Book of Messy Play Sally Featherstone (Featherstone Education 2002)

Further information and resources – music and dance

Sounds like Playing: Music and the early years curriculum Marjorie Ouvry (British Association for Early Childhood Education 2004)

Stomp Out Loud DVD (1999) – musician–dancers use everyday items to make the most amazing music sounds and rhythms

Stomp: Rhythms of the World DVD (2009) – rhythm and dance from a wide range of countries around the world

The Little Book of Dance Julie Quinn and Naomi Wager (Featherstone Books 2004)

The Little Book of Junk Music Simon MacDonald and Martha Hardy (Featherstone Education 2013)

The Little Book of Nursery Rhymes Sally Featherstone and Kerry Ingham (Featherstone Education 2002)

The Sounds Of Leaping DVD – telling the story of how children's enthusiasm for leaping is used to create a symphony, available from Sightlines Initiative's online store, www.sightlines-initiative.com (under 'Videos and DVDs')

Further information and resources – imaginative play and stories

37 Shadows: Listening to children's stories from the woods Deb Wilenski (Cambridge Curiosity and Imagination 2013) – available online or as a free downloadable booklet from www.cambridgecandi.org.uk (located under 'Current', then 'Publications')

A Place to Talk Outside Elizabeth Jarman (Featherstone Education 2009)

Bad Guys Don't Have Birthdays: Fantasy play at four Vivian Gussin Paley (University of Chicago Press 1988)

I Made a Unicorn! Open-ended play with blocks and simple materials – free downloadable PDF by Community Playthings with Tina Bruce, Lynn McNair and Sian Wyn Siencyn (2008), available from www.communityplaythings.co.uk (under 'Training Resources')

Let's Take a Storybook Outside: Exciting ways to promote outdoor creativity Ruth Ludlow (Lawrence Educational Publications 2008)

Literacy Outdoors: 50 exciting starting points for outdoor literacy experiences Ros Bayley, Helen Bromley and Lynn Broadbent (Lawrence Educational Publications 2006)

Look, the Trees Are On Fire Rising Sun Woodland Preschool project DVD – shows very imaginative use of weekly visits to a woodland site and how adults planned for 'provocations', available from Sightlines Initiative's online store, www.sightlines-initiative.com

Outdoor Banking DVD – explores how adults can support a new role-play theme outdoors, available from Wingate Nursery School and Children's Centre, www.wingatenursery.com (located under 'Training Base', then 'DVD Packages')

Sing a Song, Tell A Tale: Enriching children's experience through music, drama and movement Anni McTavish (The British Association for Early Childhood Education 2008) – a very accessible and practical guide

The Little Book of Prop Boxes for Role Play Ann Roberts (Featherstone Education 2002)
The Little Book of Small World Play Sharon Ward (Featherstone Education 2005)
The Mouse House Linda Lines, Robin Duckett and Chris Holmes – documentation of children's imaginative responses to being in a woodland over a year (Sightlines Initiative 2002)
The Small World Recipe Book: 50 exciting ideas for small world play Helen Bromley (Lawrence Educational Publications 2004)
Young Children Talking: The art of conversation and why children need to chatter Di Chilvers (British Association for Early Childhood Education 2006)

Further information and resources – suppliers

Cosy catalogue for writer's belts, writing caddies, art and weaving materials, www.cosy-direct.com
Early Excellence has a very extensive range of small-world resources, www.earlyexcellence.com
Knock on Wood (online catalogue) for world music and instruments, www.knockonwood.co.uk
Mindstretchers for world 'playground' music CDs, www.mindstretchers.co.uk
Open Ends has a mark-making wheelbarrow and an outdoor free-standing whiteboard, www.openends.co.uk
Playgarden has a boxed collection of wooden outdoor instruments, www.playgardens.co.uk
TTS Educational Supplies for robust CD players, recorders, digital cameras and video cameras suitable for outdoor use, www.tts-group.co.uk (located under 'ICT for Early Years')
Yellow Door for an outdoor writing kit designed by Helen Bromley, www.yellow-door.net

Summary

- Imagination and creativity go hand in hand and are very important for young children's well-being and all-round development.
- Taking provision for imagination and creativity outside significantly extends and enriches children's experiences because of what the outdoors has to offer that is not available indoors: the outdoors offers a wonderful environment for imaginative and creative play.
- Creative experiences outdoors include mark-making, art, drawing, pattern-making, weaving, sculpture, design, construction, woodwork, music, dance, pretend play, small-world play, story-telling, books and performance. The outdoors can offer rich and relevant opportunities in all these areas of experience that are quite different from what can be offered indoors.
- Plan for a generous environment outdoors with lots of stimulus and opportunity, continuous access to relevant resources, an emphasis on spontaneity, and flexibility in planning and provision.
- Good-quality creative and imaginative play is emergent, cannot be determined in advance and requires plenty of uninterrupted time to develop to a deep level. This requires an unhurried approach where the detail of what is going on is observed and appreciated.

- Making sure that there is opportunity and time for conversation and unpressured reflection is also important.
- Since creativity is not a tidy process, a truly creative outdoor environment is more like a work-site and likely to be somewhat chaotic and messy, so good basic organisation and routines are important.
- Children should have opportunities for extensive creative activity and play outside all through the year. Keeping warm and comfortable is vital and rain-wear works well.
- The basic resources for this area of provision need not cost much and can be easily collected into mobile containers for children to take to where they want to use them.
- The most effective resources for the development and use of imagination and expression are open-ended and versatile, so that the child can use them to represent whatever he or she wants or needs. Outdoor provision can play a significant role in supporting the development of such representational and symbolic thinking.
- The best places and equipment for imaginative play are simple and flexible in use, allowing them to be modified to suit children's current play needs. Provision for imaginative play should balance the introduction of planned role-play scenarios with children's own spontaneous play themes.
- Books and story-sharing have an important place in outdoor provision, where relevance, context and atmosphere can be greatly enhanced.

Chapter 6

Providing for construction and den play outdoors

[Children must] have the power to imprint themselves upon the landscape, endow their landscape with significance and experience their own activity as capable of transforming the environment.

(Eileen Haas, *Children in the Junkyard*, 1996)

One's mind, once stretched by a new idea, never regains its original dimensions.

(Oliver Wendell Holmes)

Why construction is so effective outdoors

Construction activity is of huge interest for young children, increasing greatly in complexity from three to seven years. The big ideas we can see children working on during construction play can be summed up as 'how does the world work?' and 'how do I fit into it?' and both are of vital interest to our avid young meaning-makers. Experiences of constructing also provide a stream of opportunities for children to feed another important need to know – that of 'what happens if…' and 'what can I make happen?' Learning and understanding that events and actions have particular consequences (cause and effect) is extremely useful for thinking scientifically and creatively, gives the child a great sense of influence and 'agency' and is also useful in developing awareness of their own (and others') safety. Because children will find plenty of space, freedom and stimuli outdoors, construction play is greatly extended by offering it as a major ingredient of your outdoor provision and children can do lots more to explore these big questions in relevant and meaningful situations.

As you will see in this chapter, construction, building and making outdoors offers huge potential for learning and development in all aspects of the curriculum for the early years. It is especially successful because it is full of moving and doing, so that it meets the way young children learn best. The greater space for construction means that we can offer big resources which invite children to work communally on a big scale. The high levels of activity and action, together with removal of constraints upon noise and mess, allow boys to engage in higher levels of social, cooperative play and dramatic play than they do indoors (see *Outdoor Play in the Early Years* by Helen Bilton, 2002, p. 70).

Do remember that taking things apart is an important aspect of construction, as 'de-constructing' is a good way to find out how things are put together. Some settings now offer 'tinkering' tables or places outside where children are provided with old (made safe) household items, such as a telephone, fan or speaker, so that they can dismantle them, examine the parts and perhaps find new combinations for putting these pieces together. Tinkering and 'messing around' with the things in their world is full of curiosity, surprise and intrigue for children, and is known to be the most effective way for learning how things work and being able to fix them (research has shown that good scientists, artists and inventors had plenty of this in their childhoods). The pioneer of the bigger idea of 'Tinkering School' in the USA, Gever Tulley, describes the process as educating children 'who see the really tough problems as puzzles, and have the tenacity, the creative resources and the creative ability to solve those puzzles' (Gever Tulley, *TEDxKids@Brussels*, 2011).

A special kind of construction is the wonderful world of den-building and this is especially important in outdoor provision. Young children have a great need for small, nurturing spaces and they can be constructed on grass, sand and tarmac, as well as amongst bushes. Dens seem to have a special appeal and to generate particular ways of playing, especially when they offer a feeling of being out of sight and a place from which to look out. Outdoor spaces so often lack softness and comfort, so this is a really effective way to add places for withdrawal, emotional security and where quieter or daunted children feel able to play. The spaces made in den and other construction play can then become whatever the child's powerfully imaginative mind wants them to be. Adults should be alert to the fact that the play that develops in dens and other 'secret' places may well derive from a child's concerns and worries (such as getting lost and being caught by baddies), and can, if well supported, be a powerful mechanism for helping them to work on personal anxieties and fears. Traditional nursery stories have

Figure 6.1 The wonderful world of den play.

been so effective because this is just what they do, and they go well with this kind of play.

Older children within this age group will also be highly motivated to make special places for imagined tiny people or things. Building on previous small-world play in the outdoors (see Chapter 5), the fantastic world of constructing fairy houses and gardens – or tree houses, caves and playgrounds for elves and goblins – opens up. Making homes for mice and other small creatures can also be of great interest and importance, drawing from concerns about their well-being and feeding emotional as well as imaginative development. A wide range of natural materials make the best resources for construction on this scale, combined with small things from the garden and home, such as flower pots and glass beads. Inspiration for making such tiny places might be found everywhere outdoors, but the most likely stimulus will come from natural spots, such as a weathered tree stump, the border under some bushes or holes between the stones in an old wall. There have been many wonderful children's storybooks over the years that adults will strongly relate to (see the booklist at the end of this chapter), and this may be an area where adults and children meaningfully work together to realise the child's ideas. For plenty of inspiration for constructing on a tiny scale with a focus on connecting children with nature, visit www.fairyhouses.com.

A final aspect of construction outdoors that should be considered is woodworking. Emerging from the traditional Froebel-inspired nursery schools in the early 1900s, woodwork was commonly seen as a core part of early childhood practice. Wood is a beautiful natural material that is, and has always been, important in so many aspects of our lives – it is not surprising that children are drawn to handling and working with it. Unfortunately, recent growing health and safety concerns have meant that new practitioners are no longer trained or confident in the safe provision of woodwork experiences, and this special area of construction is now rarely offered. This is a great and unnecessary loss – and the Forest School movement does seek to address the issue. However, woodworking is so valuable in so many ways, not least to children's sense of responsibility, trust and efficacy, that some settings are now pioneering its reintroduction into daily provision and practice, so that children can gently and gradually develop in competence, safety and success. A woodworking bench outside links well with other outdoor activities and allows more room to work in and bigger constructions to be made. Plenty of space to work in and freedom from distraction so that children can pay close attention to what they are doing are key safety requirements. Ensure children know the rules for safe use and have the necessary skills or the help they need to master new skills. Visit the website of Pete Moorhouse (http://woodworkworks.wordpress.com) for lots of practical advice, and read his excellent book *Woodwork in Early Years Education* (which is also full of inspiring images of young children at work with wood). Ensure also that children understand and come to appreciate the connection to living trees and growing wood.

Construction can take place in many ways and in most parts of outdoor spaces: different surfaces and features will inspire different types of construction, from tiny to grand scale, and spontaneous play may occur in unexpected places. To get the most out of this fantastic activity, consider how to encourage relevant kinds of construction in all aspects of your outdoor provision; for example, making cane wigwams for the growing runner beans, assembling a water wall along a fence for water play or constructing a rack for the wellington boots. So that you do not confine construction to a particular time, type or place in your outdoor area, you will need to offer a good range of suitable resources on a continuous basis and in mobile containers available from a central workshop-style base (which is likely to be your shed), adding extra resources and enhancement activities as interest arises.

Resources for construction play outdoors

There are many great resources that will invite children to build and make outdoors. As always, think about how the construction play you are providing for outside complements, links to and extends the experiences children are having indoors and at home. You will want to build upon previous experience while offering opportunities that are new and that make the most of what the outdoors brings: space and scale – from miniscule to grand; features, surfaces and spaces

Figure 6.2 A well-prepared woodworking environment is full of motivation and possibility.

that make a very different environment to indoors; materials and resources that cannot be offered indoors; stimuli from around and beyond the outdoor space, from home or from the local area.

Open-ended resources that do not have a fixed purpose for play and which can be used in many ways by children will offer lots of potential for building and construction. These resources will also be used for many other activities and will therefore constitute the mainstays of your continuous provision outdoors. Large items, such as boxes, crates and guttering, will encourage collaborative group construction, but remember to provide resources for small-scale and individual constructions too. It is important to begin with simple materials and simple ideas, so as not to overwhelm children (and remember that some three-year-olds may not have made dens or constructions before), and to have an abundant supply of a few good resources (such as boxes and crates), rather than lots of different types. Add gradually over the year so that children can keep building on well-embedded experience and knowledge. If construction is offered as continuous provision, and children have long periods of time outdoors everyday, their ideas will grow alongside their capacities for successfully making them happen.

Give particular thought to the materials and methods you offer children for connecting, joining and fixing things together. Children with a schematic interest in 'connection' will be strongly drawn to this aspect of construction, but all children will learn a great deal through the challenge of making things fix together sufficiently well for their ideas to be realised. The technology of joining holds a great amount of fascination, and children will need to repeat again and again, and to work over time in order to both master the techniques and understand how they work. Many connecting experiences will be available through how the building materials themselves can be made to join with each other – such as down-pipes fitting into the holes in milk crates. Many additional joining experiences can be introduced through the specific resources supplied for the purpose, especially for den-making (see 'Resources for joining and fixing' below). Starting simply, slowly add to the range and increase the complexity of fixing resources across the year, so that children build a good repertoire of knowledge and skills.

When selecting the resources you will make continuously available, try to ensure that children always have opportunities to:

- construct on a grand scale, such as creating bridges, towers and obstacle courses;
- construct for real purposes, such as making temporary seating with tyres and planks;
- make dens and secret spaces;
- make tiny structures, such as with twigs and pebbles;
- make things to use, such as woodwork or instruments;
- construct in many places, using features such as sand, soil, slopes and the climbing frame;
- construct in role-play scenarios, such as a builder's yard in the sand pit with ropes and pulleys;
- experience a wide range of mechanisms for connecting and fixing items together;
- play in or with their constructions once made.

Some of the best things to construct with

Resources for construction outdoors

Milk and bread crates (check daily for broken parts)
Tyres (ensure clean and no metal protrusions)
Sections of guttering and down-pipes – in a range of diameters and lengths
Sections of hard and soft plastic piping in a range of diameters (try plumbing suppliers)
Large hollow wooden blocks (from *Community Playthings* and *NES Arnold*)
Short lengths of planking, such as for outdoor decking
Large washing powder boxes (taped closed ensuring no loose powder)
Cardboard boxes – use as 3D and opened out as large sheets
Large and small plastic flower pots

Bricks (small real bricks, such as block paving – ensure edges are not sharp)

Soft play blocks

Plastic drums (such as water dispenser bottles – any container that previously held chemicals must be rigorously cleaned and sealed)

Cardboard carpet-roll tubes (from carpet stores and carpet layers)

Bamboo canes (tape ends to protect eyes), lengths of 2.5 cm diameter doweling

Broom handles – best with plastic top with hole for ropes, willow poles with a hole drilled in one end (from *Muddy Faces*)

Roll of plastic-coated garden mesh fencing (from garden centres)

Wood off-cuts, tree trunk slices, branches cut into short lengths

Clothes airers/clothes horse (old-fashioned wooden ones are ideal, but remove metal hinges to avoid trapped fingers) (*Open Ends* supplies one with Velcro strap hinges)

Large pieces of fabric, blankets, sheets, net and other curtains, lengths of muslin

Tarpaulin, camouflage net (from army surplus stores)

Empty 0.5 and 1 ton aggregate bags (from builders' merchants)

Clear market stall cover (from *Muddy Faces*), big plastic sheeting (from a DIY store)

Shower curtains

Greenhouse shading (from garden centres) – look for more than 1 m wide, decorators' cover sheets (from DIY stores)

Cargo netting (from scrapstores)

Small parachute, pop-up tents, fishing shelters, beach windbreak

Garden parasol (waterproof), parasol base

Carpet tiles or pieces, plastic-backed picnic blanket, beach mat

A range of long and short, thick and thin ropes, washing line, simple pulleys (from chandlers/boat shop)

Hooks in walls and fences to provide attachment points for ropes

Plastic cones, plastic cable reels and wooden cable drums

Steering wheels (from scrap yards)

Buckets, wheelbarrows, bikes and carts for transporting materials

Natural materials, such as shells, pebbles, sticks, moss, twigs, etc.

Woodwork bench and simple (but real) tools

Untreated and unpainted soft wood off-cuts (pine, fir, lime, cedar, redwood are suitable; avoid plywood and MDF)

Nails, screws, bottle tops, wood glue

Safety glasses, safety gloves (where necessary) (from *Muddy Faces* and *Open Ends*)

Spirit level, rules and winding tape measures

Resources for joining and fixing

Trolley with pull-out trays or tool boxes for organising mobile joining and fixing materials

String, garden twine, garden twist ties

Soft twisty plant ties (from DIY stores)

Masking tape, carpet or duct tape, parcel tape, electrical tape, etc.

Velcro strips

Elastic bungee cords (from car accessories stores), ball bungees (from *Muddy Faces*)

Scissors

Thick elastic bands, treasury tags

Tent pegs and mallet

Pegs – normal and large sizes, duvet/quilt pegs (from *Betterware* and *Lakeland*)

Shower curtain rings and suckers

Carabiners – range of sizes (from climbing stores)

Garden cane holders (for making bean wigwams – a wide range is available from garden centres and *Cosy*)

Figure 6.3 Bread crates make superb construction resources.

Storing and organising resources for construction outdoors

Children need to know what is available for construction, how the materials can be used (and any limitations on this), where to find particular resources and where to return them to when finished. If the resources can cope with getting wet, such as crates and guttering, they can be stacked outside, leaving valuable space in your shed: an occasional wash down with the hose will delight children interested in water play. Fabric items are best stored indoors, to prevent damp and mildew, so find containers that make transporting them outside easy: a laundry basket might be just the thing as children can easily see and access the contents, and can work together to carry it. Resources made of cardboard are easy to replace, so can be stored in a shed and allowed to gradually deteriorate, being used in different ways as they fall apart. In contrast, expensive wooden blocks need a good wheeled trolley as you will want to store these indoors or in a good shed.

Make sure resources are stored in the shed in a way that makes them as easy as possible to find, bring out and return – how you do this will depend on the size and shape of the items. A shallow but wide shed with doors that open up fully will make resources easy to see, locate, get out and put away. As well as crates and laundry baskets on shelves, consider hooks for individual items and bins for long items; elastic cords attached to hooks in the wall can help to keep things in place. Laminated photographs attached to containers will show children what is in that particular container. If the images used are those taken by children of things they have made themselves with these resources, this will give the labels further meaning, also reminding them of things made previously or providing new ideas for constructions.

Supporting play in and with structures children have made

So much more will be gained for both well-being and learning if children have plenty of opportunity to develop other play with their constructions: time and supportive adults are perhaps the resources children most need for really effective construction play outside. Children are unlikely to invest effort in constructing something unless they feel that they will have time to make the use of it they have in mind, and short periods of play outdoors are just not conducive to deep and complex play. When children have lots of time to build dens, they have been

Figure 6.4 The range of constructions children make outdoors is surprisingly wide.

observed to build a basic structure, then play with it for a while, then to decorate, extend or otherwise embellish their dens, and then to play in it some more. This cycle of construction and imaginative play can continue over time if children have opportunities to return to their structure over the day or even over the week, so it is well worth taking a new look at your provision to see if constructions must always be cleared away.

The range of constructions children might make outdoors and the variety of activities they may then want to follow through in or with them is surprisingly wide, but many of the resources you have available for other aspects of provision will offer what is needed:

- role-play scenarios, such as a builders' yard with construction hats, cones and wheeled vehicles or home DIY with tools and tape measure in a tool box;
- home play and fantasy play, adding a torch and binoculars to your resources for imaginative play;
- ropes to create a working drawbridge for the castle, spades for digging a ditch in the sand to fill for a moat;
- pulleys (from hardware and sailing shops) and ropes, with paper and pens to make message systems or with baskets to transport other items to and from the den, or with buckets to add to the building site;
- bikes with trailers, carts and other transport vehicles to carry building materials to and from the construction site, gloves and high-visibility vest for the lorry driver;
- small-world resources for play with small-scale structures created, such as play people, fairies, trucks, dinosaurs and natural materials – a wheeled trolley with pull-out drawers is ideal for making these resources available;
- cushions and blankets for making a comfortable place to rest;
- puppets and books to tell stories in the special place made (see booklists below);
- music to create an appropriate atmosphere for the emerging play theme, or simply to relax to in the den;
- real food for a snack in the den;
- clipboards to plan the construction or to draw and map out the resulting structure;
- mark-making materials to make signs (such as the name of the den or safety advice, such as 'Danger! – hole in road'), directions or pathways, etc. Again, a trolley with pull-out drawers kitted out with pens, chalk, paper and joining materials allows these materials to be taken wherever they are required;
- things to decorate the construction or den with, such as ribbons, strips of fabric, bells, big felt pens, chalk, paint, old CDs, natural materials, wool, etc.;
- a performance with the instruments made or a place outside, such as the branches of a tree, to decorate with the woodwork items made;
- real building materials to explore closely, together with examples provided by wooden and brick buildings in the outdoor space or locality;

- a camera for children and adults to take photographs of the work in progress – these could be displayed or made into sequence or story books which children will return to many times.

Getting the most out of construction play across the curriculum

The best kind of provision supports all areas of the child's development through holistic, joined-up experiences, and a good judge of the value of an experience is to examine how broadly it 'covers' (or rather uncovers or reveals) the curriculum. Construction outdoors is a truly holistic aspect of provision, especially when children have plenty of time to develop their play and it is supported by adults who can notice, capture and build upon the things children are showing interest in. Let's take a look at some of the potential for learning and development that well-supported construction play has to offer the child.

Emotional and social development

When children are following their own interests and satisfying their strong urge to find out by taking apart and putting together, they develop positive dispositions, such as taking an interest, being deeply involved, making plans, concentrating, trying things out, making mistakes and persisting with challenge and difficulty. They will need just the right support from adults to successfully build these desirable approaches to life.

Because there are many opportunities for big-scale construction and group role play, building partners will be learning how to work together, negotiate and collaborate. Play in dens is especially important for supporting emotional wellbeing outdoors, giving children soft places with feelings of enclosure, security and nurture, and a place where they can regulate the amount of interaction they have with others.

Communication and the foundations of literacy

In both the communal and solitary activities of construction, there are lots of motivational contexts for the use of language, language development and the introduction of new vocabulary. Children often welcome the (sensitive) help of adults to achieve their plans, so staff will find many opportunities both to support conversation and discussion with open-ended questions as they work together and to model language use by responding to children's comments. All construction activity can provoke episodes of sustained, shared talk and thinking between children and with adults because of the shared purpose. Big-scale, group construction is especially rich in provoking the use of language for both communication and thinking and a whole host of sophisticated communication skills: turning the imagined visual idea into words, articulating and describing what the idea is, conveying it to others so that they understand and want to cooperate, negotiating the plan, problem-solving in order to achieve the plan and the complex language used when playing imaginatively in the construction made. In addition, there is all the new vocabulary specific to building, materials and structures, such as brick, wall, corner, build, strong, wobbly, inside, balance, fall-down, mortar and so on.

Construction play is also full of reasons to make marks or use emergent writing, such as drawing a diagram of the construction or making a sign to warn that hard hats must be worn. There will be many stories to make up and many more to read – construction has strong links to all kinds of imaginative play and factual books showing how things are made are of particular interest to boys.

Movement and physical development

Construction can be a very active and physical occupation, especially with large construction items and when boys are involved. Children will be lifting, carrying, bending, placing, stretching, manoeuvring, holding, pulling and pushing; all of which are excellent for developing muscles, strength, coordination, body aware-ness, spatial awareness and motor planning and control (praxis). They will be using their fingers for manipulating and joining, developing dexterity and hand–eye coordination, and they will also be using the senses in a joined-up way, so

Figure 6.5 Logical and creative thinking are working side by side in the child's mind.

helping integration of sensory pathways in the brain. Whole-body work activates and energises the brain and gives input for thinking at many levels, so that the learning experience is much deeper and long-lasting (we think in all the ways we experience). Remember too that all this energetic activity can be balanced by having a cosy snack or story in the den that has just been made.

Understanding of how the world works, including mathematical thinking, technology and design

Construction play helps children in their quest to know about their world: what it is made up of, what things do and what they can make them do. They can explore and experiment with materials and how they can be put together and taken apart. While constructing, they will be discovering 'what happens if…' and about cause, effect and consequences ('If I do this, then that happens'). When building a tower or a wall they can, just like true scientists, ask questions, have ideas about how things work (theories), experiment with those ideas, predict what will happen, and then refine and improve their theories with this new information. All this does not merely develop knowledge and understanding about the external world; it also actually builds the thinking processes and capacities for reasoning and learning in the brain. Active, relevant and motivational experiences are also how the capacities for self-regulation and for managing thinking are best developed.

During construction activity, children will be getting first hand and 'felt' meanings for lots of concepts, such as gravity, weight, balance and friction. They will be learning design skills and technical knowledge about how to join things together, and they will have to identify and solve problems when their construction ideas do not work and to evaluate the structure once they have succeeded in making it. Make use of your locality as it is quite likely that some building work is going on nearby. Take the children out frequently to watch, take photographs and discuss what is happening, then offer the children the opportunity to create a relevant role-play scenario if they show interest. Be sure to make the most of the experiences children bring from home. You might have a small expert if some kind of construction is going on or a parent works in the industry. For example, a three-year-old who laid all the books out side by side on the ground explained that he was 'building a patio like Daddy'.

Many of the major schemas that occupy young children are naturally supported in construction activities, such as connecting, transporting, lines and trajectories, in and out, placing, going through a boundary, enclosure and containment. A group of children with similar or compatible schematic interests are likely to work well together on a large construction and those with very different interests might well come into conflict, so being 'schema aware' will be very useful in planning and providing useful support! Schemas have strong relationships to mathematical development, and construction play provides endless opportunities to really get a feel for shape, edges and boundaries, space, size and fit, position (inside, under, behind), matching and sorting, comparison (more, less, longer, thicker) and measurement (how high, how long), and to use the relevant vocabulary when it means something to the children. A child can get a strong, embodied meaning of space and 'inside' when their body is surrounded by a construction they have just made for themselves.

Creative, aesthetic and expressive development

While deeply involved in constructing, logical and creative thinking are truly working side by side in the child's mind. Much construction play involves creative thinking: exploring the way materials can be used, using previous experience and knowledge to apply to a new situation and putting things together to create new combinations. Children are also visualising in their minds and then expressing their ideas, thoughts and feelings, whether it be with the overall plan of what it is they want to build or with a specific problem that needs to be worked out. Sometimes, children will have an idea to start with and can make drawings to help them plan it. Often though, ideas will arise as children start to play since creativity usually grows better in a playful, emergent and non-demanding situation – it is so often more productive not to have too much of a preconceived project or product in mind (especially from the adults). Many children will,

Figure 6.6 Space, materials and time must all be generously available for complex construction to take place.

however, want to make drawings, paintings or photo-shoots of constructions they have enjoyed making.

There is a great deal of stimuli for the child's imagination while they are engaged in building or making and much potential for imaginative or creative play to follow on, such as fantasy play, role play and playing instruments they have made. Observe your children attentively to catch the sparks that will help you fire further creative activity.

Gender differences in construction play outdoors

You may well notice significant differences in the way boys and girls undertake construction activity. Research into gender differences in children's use of the outdoors showed that boys played with the more active equipment and girls tended to stay with the quieter home-type play (Cullen, 1993, in Bilton, *Outdoor Play in the Early Years*, 2002, p. 74). Boys tended to modify the landscape more frequently while girls' modifications were more likely to be in their imaginations, such as turning branches into shelves. Boys tended to build the outer parts of a building – the walls, windows and roofs – and girls worked on the interior design – tables, chairs and decorations (Hart, 1978, in Bilton, *Outdoor Play in the Early Years*, 2002, p. 74). Significantly, when boys came across girls building, they would take over and the girls would become subservient. These findings are now 20–35 years old and it may be that increased focus on avoiding gender stereotyping has helped to reduce the gender differences in construction play both indoors and out – and indeed some Forest School practitioners report less stereotypical play behaviour in a woodland environment with natural materials rather than toys. Clearly further research into this issue with respect to play outdoors and what factors seem to influence how children play there will be valuable, along with recognition that boys and girls may have different things that they need to process through their play.

They do, however, show how vital it is to observe, evaluate and adjust both what you provide and how you support it to ensure girls as well as boys have opportunities that appeal to them and that allow them to retain leading roles. Girls often enjoy having an adult to talk to, so are more likely to engage with construction activities, such as woodwork, when an adult is fully involved.

Evaluating your provision for construction play

It is very useful to closely monitor what is happening in particular areas of your outdoor provision so that you can periodically evaluate how well that aspect is working for all your children, and consider how it might be made more effective. As an example, some questions to ask yourselves about your outdoor construction play, perhaps at a staff meeting, are given below to help you think about just one of the main ingredients of outdoor provision. It can be enormously beneficial to take a similar in-depth look at each of the main ingredients of outdoor provision, spread out over the year. Different members of staff could take the lead on different aspects, so as to spread the task and give everyone a stake in the provision outside.

First, use observations everyone has made about what children do (or do not do) and how their play is stimulated and supported, to consider how effective current provision really is. Then discuss and agree what you could do to further develop it. Do not forget to ask the children for their thoughts, feelings and ideas, as this will greatly increase your understanding of the play, give you ideas for development that you as adults would not have thought of and give the children a great sense of responsibility and ownership of the outdoor provision.

- Which children get involved in construction in your outdoor area? What is it that appeals to those who are engaged?
- Are there some who do not find it interesting: why might this be and what can you do to engage them?
- Which resources work particularly well for construction: would more of these be valuable?
- Which construction activities and resources interest boys and which interest girls: how could you increase their interest and involvement?
- What aspects of the early years curriculum are being strongly supported through your construction activities: how could you share this with parents?
- How could you further develop construction opportunities to bring in other areas of learning in motivational ways?
- Do all staff enjoy supporting construction activity and do they find it easy to take an appropriate and effective role: what could you do to help this?
- Does construction activity interfere with any other aspect of your outdoor provision: what needs to be done to improve this?
- Are there any other issues arising from observations, comments from home and discussions with the children?

Young children's most powerful learning is accompanied by the expression of wonder, excitement, enjoyment, fun and pleasure.

(Marion Dowling)

Rhymes and songs

Humpty Dumpty
Hickory Dickory Dock
If I Had a Hammer
London Bridge is Falling Down
Peter Hammers with One Hammer
The Animals Went in Two by Two
The House That Jack Built

Children's books to support construction

A Sailing Boat in the Sky Quentin Blake (Red Fox 2003)
Abel's Moon Shirley Hughes (Red Fox 2002)
Castles Colin Thompson (Red Fox 2007)
★*Castles* Maggie Freeman and Cliff Moon (Collins Educational 2005)
Clancy & Millie and the Very Fine House Libby Gleeson and Freya Blackwood (Little Hare 2009)
★*Find Out About Wood* Henry Pluckrose (Franklin Watts 2002)
★*Iggy Peck Architect* Andrea Beaty and David Roberts (Harry N. Abrams 2007)
In the Castle Anna Milbourne and Benjie Davies (Usborne Publishing 2011)
★*Junk Collector School* Adam Dahlin and Emma Akerman (R&S Books 2007)
Once There Was a House, a House that was a Home Alex T. Smith (Scholastic Children's Books 2009)
Once Upon a Tide Tony Mitton and Selina Young (Picture Corgi 2006)
★*Roxaboxen* Alice McLerran and Barbara Cooney (Simon & Schuster 2004)
Seaside Buildings Paul Humphrey (Franklin Watts 2006)
★*See Inside Castles* Katie Daynes and David Hancock (Usborne Publishing 2005)
The Boy Who Built the Boat Ross Mueller and Craig Smith (Allen & Unwin 2010)
The Den Adam Stower (Bloomsbury Publishing 2005)
The House that Jill Built Phyllis Root and Delphone Durand (Candlewick Press 2005)
The Lighthouse Keeper's Lunch Ronda and David Armitage (Scholastic Children's Books 1994)
The Three Little Pigs: An architectural tale Stephen Guarnaccia (Harry N. Abrams 2010)
The Three Little Wolves and the Big Bad Pig Eugene Trivizas and Helen Oxenbury (Egmont Books Ltd 2003)
Three Bears Cliff Wright (Templar Publishing 2006)
Whatever Next? Jill Murphy (Macmillan Children's Books 1995)
There are many appropriate factual books, such as on how things are made; machines and buildings. Try Dorling Kindersley (www.dorlingkindersley-uk.co.uk)
DIY and building magazines, with lots of full colour images.

Children's books about houses and homes

★*A House Is a House for Me* Mary Ann Hoberman and Betty Fraser (Puffin Books 2007)
Harry's Home Catharine and Laurence Anholt (Orchard 2009)
Home Alex T. Smith (Scholastic 2009)
Home (Around the world) Kate Perry and Oxfam (Frances Lincoln Children's Books 2007)
Homes (Around the world) Margaret Hall (Heinemann Library 2003)
Houses and Homes (Around the world series) Ann Morris (William Morrow 2007)
★*Houses and Homes (Where you live)* Ruth Nason (Franklin Watts 2010)
Little House by the Sea Benedict Blathwyt (Red Fox 1994)

Children's books to support play in and with dens and other constructions

Bear Snores On Karma Wilson and Jane Chapman (Simon & Schuster 2005)
Ben's Box Michael Foreman, David A. Carter and David Pelham (Piggy Toes Press 1997)

Beryl's Box Lisa Taylor and Penny Dann (Picture Lions 1993)

★*Duncan's Tree House* Amanda Vesey (Collins Picture Lions 1992)

Goat and Donkey in the Great Outdoors Simon Puttock and Russell Julian (OUP Oxford 2008)

Goldilocks and the Three Bears Lauren Child and Emily Jenkins (Puffin 2009)

Harry's Box Angela McAllister and Jenny Jones (Bloomsbury Publishing 2005)

I Thought I Saw a Dinosaur! Emma Dodd (Templar Publishing 2007)

Mr Bear's Holiday Debi Gliori (Orchard 2007)

Not a Box Antoinnette Portis (HarperFestival 2011)

Picnic Mick Inkpen (Hodder Children's Books, Little Kippers 2001)

Rosy's Visitors Judy Hindley and Helen Craig (Walker Books 2002)

Sally's Secret Shirley Hughes (Red Fox 1992)

Sleep Tight, Little Bear Martin Wadell and Barbara Firth (Walker Books 2006)

Ten in the Den John Butler (Orchard 2006)

The Bear's Winter House John Yeoman and Quentin Blake (Andersen Press 2009)

★*The Garden* Dyan Sheldon and Gary Blythe (Hutchinson 1993)

★*The Green Ship* Quentin Blake (Red Fox 2000)

The House that Jack Built Diana Mayo (Barefoot Books 2006)

The Tin Forest Helen Ward and Wayne Anderson (Templar Publishing 2009)

We're Going on a Bear Hunt Michael Rosen and Helen Oxenbury (Walker Books 2001)

Whatever Next! Jill Murphy (Macmillan Children's Books 2007)

Children's books to support den play to deal with fears

Can't You Sleep, Little Bear? Martin Waddell and Barbara Firth (Walker Books 2005)

Follow that Bear if You Dare Claire Freedman and Alison Edgson (Little Tiger Press 2008)

In the Dark, Dark Woods Jessica Souhami (Frances Lincoln Children's Books 2007)

In the Woods Chris Wormell (Red Fox 2004)

Into the Forest Anthony Browne (Walker Books 2005)

Kipper's Monster Mick Inkpen (Hodder Children's Books 2008)

★*Little Mouse's Big Book of Fears* Emily Gravett (Macmillan Children's Books 2008)

Scaredy Squirrel at Night Melanie Watt (Catnip 2010)

The Gruffalo Julia Donaldson and Axel Scheffler (Macmillan Children's Books 1999)

The Secret Cave Richard Hamilton and Helen Lanzrein (Orchard 2007)

Children's books to support small-world construction play

★*Children of the Forest* Elsa Beskow (Floris Books 1987) – a Swedish story first published in 1910

Fairy Houses Tracy Kane (Light Beams Publishing 2001)

Fairy Houses and Beyond! Tracy Kane and Barry Kane (Light Beams Publishing 2008)

Fairy Houses ... Everywhere! Barry Kane and Tracy Kane (Light Beams Publishing 2006)

Fairy House Handbook Liz Gardner Walsh (Down East Books 2012)

Fairy Houses of the Maine Coast Maureen Heffernan and Robert Mitchell (Down East Books 2010)

Fairy Houses … Unbelievable: A photographic tour Barry Kane and Tracy Kane (Light Beams Publishing 2012)

The Adventures of Mrs Pepperpot Alf Proysen and Hilda Offen (Red Fox 2010)

The Amazing Mrs Pepperpot Alf Proysen and Hilda Offen (Red Fox 2011)

The Bog Baby Jeanne Willis and Gwen Millward (Puffin 2008)

The Complete Book of the Flower Fairies Cicely Mary Barker (Frederick Warne 2002)

The Complete Borrowers Mary Norton (Puffin 2007)

The Complete Brambly Hedge Jill Barklem (HarperCollins Children's Books 2011)

The King of Tiny Things Jeanne Willis and Gwen Millward (Puffin 2010)

The Minpins Roald Dahl and Patrick Benson (Puffin 2008)

The Snail House Allan Ahlberg and Gillian Tyler (Walker Books 2000)

The Story of the Butterfly Children Sibylle von Olfers (Floris Books 2009) – also the story of the root children; snow children; and wind children (first published in German from 1905 to 1920)

Further information and resources – further reading

Beautiful Stuff: Learning with found materials Cathy Weisman Topal and Lella Gandini (Davis Publications 1999) – although not outdoors, this is well worth reading, and emphasises taking things slowly

Exploring Learning: Young children and blockplay Pat Gura (ed.; Paul Chapman Publishing 1992)

Fascination of Earth: Wood whittling Claire Warden (Mindstretchers 2012)

I Made a Unicorn! Open-ended play with blocks and simple materials – free downloadable PDF by Community Playthings with Tina Bruce, Lynn McNair and Sian Wyn Siencyn (2008), available from www.communityplaythings.co.uk (under 'Training Resources')

Resources for Early Learning: Children, adults and stuff Pat Gura (Sage Publications 1996)

Secret Spaces, Imaginary Places: Creating your own worlds for play Elin McCoy (Prentice Hall 1986)

Teacher Tom blog site for many wonderful posts on woodworking and tinkering for young children in a community pre-school in Seattle, USA, at http://teachertomsblog.blogspot.co.uk

The Little Book of Bricks and Boxes Clare Beswick (Featherstone Education 2003)

The Little Book of Woodwork Terry Gould and Linda Morts (Featherstone Education 2012)

Tinkering School – watch a four-minute TED talk via www.ted.com, *Gever Tulley: Life lessons through tinkering* (2009), or a longer (17-minute) version via www.youtube.com, *TEDxKids@Brussels – Gever Tulley – Tinkering School* (2011), and find information about the full-time tinkering school *Brightworks* in San Francisco, USA, at http://sfbrightworks.org, where the motto is 'everything is interesting, we can create anything'

Understanding Young Children's Learning Through Play: Building playful pedagogies Pat Broadhead and Andy Burt (Routledge 2012)

Woodshop for Kids: 52 woodworking projects kids can build Jack McKee (Hands On Books 2005) – aimed at children of four years old onwards; project oriented but useful information (North American)

Woodwork in Early Years Education Pete Moorhouse (2012), working with Filton Avenue Nursery School – fabulous resource for early childhood educators, full of colour images; order from www.petemoorhouse.co.uk/education/woodwork-book

Woodworking for Young Children Patsy Skeen and Anita P. Garner (National Association for the Education of Young Children 1984)

Woodworkworks website – dedicated to promoting and supporting woodworking in the early years, http://woodworkworks.wordpress.com. The author, Pete Moorhouse, also offers training to early years educators (information is on his website, www.petemoorhouse.co.uk/education)

Further information and resources – source material

Bent Objects: The secret life of everyday things Terry Border (Running Press 2009)

Faerie Houses Wall Calendar 2013 Sally J. Smith (Pomegranate Communications 2012) – use images for display indoors and laminate for outdoor use

Fairie-ality Style: A sourcebook of inspiration from nature David Ellwand (Walker Books 2009)

Fairy Houses Wall Calendar 2013 Amy Wilton (Down East Books 2012) – use images for display indoors and laminate for outdoor use

Global Model Village: The international street art of Slinkachu Slinkachu (Boxtree 2012) – striking change of perspectives through tiny world art (take care: some images are not suitable for young children)

Hundertwasser Architecture Calendar 2013 Freidensreich Hundertwasser (Korsh Adolf Verlag 2012)

Little People in the City: The street art of Slinkachu Slinkachu (Boxtree 2008) – striking change of perspectives through tiny world art (take care: some images are not suitable for young children)

Look the Trees Are on Fire – The Rising Sun Woodland Preschool DVD from Sightlines Initiative, www.sightlines-initiative.com, has good sequences of children constructing in the woodland and following on back at nursery

Master of Illusion Calendar 2013 – the art of Rob Gonsalves (Sellers 2012)

Milk Crate Sculpture – there is an amazing amount of art and design works using crates. Try Google Images and search under 'milk crate sculpture' as a starting point

Scrapstores are growing all over the world, with a huge range of materials suitable for outdoor construction and play – find the UK directory at www.scrapstoresuk.org

Supporting Young Children's Sustained Shared Thinking: An exploration – training DVD produced by Marion Dowling for the British Association for Early Childhood Education, which includes an excellent sequence of children making a willow structure. Available from Early Education, www.early-education.org.uk

The Amusement Park for Birds – video from Reggio Emilia, in which children designed and built an outdoor amusement park for the birds who come to their playground (Reggio Children 1992), available from www.sightlines-initiative.com

The Little Book of Little Gardens Steve Wheen (Dokument Press 2012) – a great stimulus for tiny living gardens in ordinary but surprising urban places

The Way Things Go – a really remarkable 'ingeniously choreographed' DVD of endless cause and effect, by Peter Fischili and David Weiss (2006)

Further information and resources – suppliers

Cosy catalogue has a great range of good resources, including recycled crates and tyres, www.cosydirect.com

Early Excellence has a building and construction collection, a den play collection and small, real woodworking tools, www.earlyexcellence.com

Mindstretchers online shop has shelter making and small, real woodworking resources, www.mindstretchers.co.uk

Muddy Faces online shop has an excellent range of den-making and play resources and small, real woodworking tools, www.muddyfaces.co.uk

Open Ends online shop has woodworking tools and benches and a den kit with old-fashioned clothes airer, www.openends.co.uk

Summary

- Construction play is of great interest to young children as it helps them to find out about their world in the ways they most like to learn: through moving, doing and using their whole body.
- A wide range of construction activities are possible outdoors, stimulated and supported by the special nature of the outdoor environment.
- The freedom outdoors for invention, movement, using large resources and taking up lots of room means that construction can happen on a very satisfying large scale outdoors. There is, however, also a great deal of stimulation and possibility for constructing on a tiny scale outside, working with natural materials and drawing on young children's fascination for the miniscule side of life.
- Deconstructing, messing around and 'tinkering' are important aspects of construction play in the early years and are critical for innovation in the design process. The outdoors lends itself well to supporting such 'messy' play.
- Using wood as a special material for construction is highly valuable in early childhood education. Increasing the confidence, skills and enthusiasm of practitioners for supporting safe exploration in woodwork would open up a neglected but wonderful aspect of construction play outdoors.
- Children need lots of time to construct and then to play in or with the structures they have made; short periods of outdoor play do not allow children to get deeply involved in such activity.
- Well-resourced and supported construction play is a remarkably holistic experience for children, with the potential to support a great deal of learning in all areas of the early years curriculum.
- Construction play can take place in many ways and in most parts of the outdoor space, and can also be part of other aspects of provision outdoors, including constructing for real and useful purposes.
- The best resources for construction play outdoors are open-ended and versatile, with no predetermined purpose or use. Big resources encourage collaborative construction activity on a large scale.

- Resources for construction play should be constantly available to support both planned and spontaneous ideas and interests, and are best organised in mobile containers in a central workshop-style base.
- Adults can take many roles in construction play, from interacting closely in order to scaffold children's language, thinking and skills, to supporting 'from a distance' through observation and planning: this range of roles is vital for making the most of this fantastic aspect of outdoor provision.
- Keeping a close eye on what children are doing and saying so that provision can be evaluated is very important in ensuring that provision outdoors is as good as it can be.

Chapter 7

Providing outdoor experiences beyond the garden gate

What this chapter is about

- Why go out of the garden gate?
- What does the world beyond the gate offer children?
- Preparing to go out beyond the setting
- Resources to enable excursions into the locality
- What might children notice and be interested in?
- Further afield – where else might you go?
- Getting the most out of your local excursions
- The boundaries of the setting – letting the outside in
- A seasonal outdoor alphabet
- Children's books
- Further information and resources

What the world needs now is reckless curiosity.

(Gever Tulley, quoting Andrew Bird)

When you teach a child something you take away forever his chance of discovering it for himself.

(Jean Piaget)

Why go out of the garden gate?

Like most of the children of my generation, from the age of five or six, I walked home from school every day (sometimes with a sibling but more often alone), taking my time to meander slowly, noticing everything along the way and frequently gathering a handful of the wild flowers growing in the verges as a gift for my mum. The distance was probably around half a mile, but it could take any amount of time – I have no sense now of there ever being a need to hurry. This journey is strong in my memory; 50 years on I can still see the individual sections of the route, the nature-filled edges of these paths and roads, and even feel the sensation of becoming thoroughly drenched when it was raining. A generation later, some of my favourite memories of being with my daughter as a two-year-old are of the daily walk we made together coming home from her morning nursery. We travelled this very familiar route at her pace and on her agenda, so that the ten-minute walk going usually took more like an hour coming back. She was very attentive to all that was around her, from watching ants going in and out of the pavement cracks to naming the letter shapes on car number plates and street signs (pavement-level fire hydrants and gas pipe markers being her favourite). She also loved to collect bits of 'treasure', such as the red and yellow fragments of broken vehicle tail lights. Going at this intensely curious young child's pace, tuning into what she found intriguing and sharing her fascination and focus had such a lot of value for both of us, in so many ways – especially in terms of our relationship with each other.

Young children are biologically programmed to be curious so that they can find out about their world and become able to operate safely and effectively in it – what is in this world, what does it do, what does it do to me, how do I fit into it, what can it do and what can I make it do? The two key aspects of their world that children are so keen to make sense of are the real physical world – earth, water, rocks, plants, animals, light, gravity, forces, weather, natural processes and so on – and the real human world – people, relationships, variety, what people do, how they interact, the roles they take and what it means to be human. We bring as much of this as we can into the indoor classroom but, as we have seen, this can be a very limited experience compared to providing it outside. We also aim to offer a rich range of real experiences for children in our provision outdoors in the garden – but we are still missing an enormous amount of the full range of possibilities that children need in order to find out as much as they can about their world.

The streets and locality immediately outside your garden or outdoor area has incredible potential for children's learning in all areas that is just waiting to be harvested! By taking children into this *additional layer* of outdoor provision, the possibilities for engagement, involvement, thinking and learning really are endless, and the material that then becomes available for exploring, investigating, playing and creating back in the setting, indoors and outdoors, is both abundant and rich. This practice was once not only common but expected in early years settings, and still is in many traditional nursery schools. However, factors associated with perceived health and safety issues, staff deployment and logistics, risk aversion and the weight of risk management paperwork are making this an increasingly rare or very limited aspect of current provision in most settings in the UK. While it is understandable that going outside the setting has appeared to have become more difficult (or impossible) to operate, the consequences of losing this practice are wide-ranging and profound, and we really do need to rethink these limitations with a more proactive attitude. Considering the immediate locality outside the boundaries of your grounds to be an additional layer of your outdoor provision, complementing the on-site indoor and outdoor provision, will add a whole new layer of opportunities for rich experience, development and learning which these areas are simply not capable of providing.

Most young children spend much less time in the local environment than even a generation ago, so experiences in local places where they might not otherwise go are an important component of what you can offer at nursery or school. Critically, even when children are in their locality or community, it is often with a parent or carer who is in a hurry or not able to slow down to the child's pace, or who is carrying out tasks that spare little room for diversion to respond to the child's moment-to-moment interests or desires. Perhaps the child is also in a pushchair or car seat for much of this time! Unhurried, slow-paced, child-focused and very local excursions with a very small group of children provide some magical times for children – and for the adults walking with them. This is the time to really get to know your children, find out what they are capable of, and discover all sorts of things about their lives. A teacher at Bognor Regis Nursery School and Children's Centre said recently that, while they are walking down the street to play on the beach, the children talk about 'anything and everything – you even get to know that their Mum likes Mamma Mia'. You may have gone out with a few children to post a letter – but if you do not make it to the post box, it does not matter at all.

Figure 7.1 Unhurried, slow-paced, child-focused and very local excursions provide some magical times for children.

What does the world beyond the gate offer children?

The key to working with this additional layer of outdoor provision is that it is seen as just that – a further area of your outdoor space that has a particular character, feels different to the other parts of the garden and provides a unique range of special opportunities, ways to be and things to do, and which you use a lot (preferably daily), with all of the children. With this approach, children visit this part of the provision frequently and repeatedly over a long period of time, so that they become familiar with it, comfortable in it, able to attend to more and more of its details and able to explore their relationship with it. When this happens, children have the opportunity to:

- get to know their locality and develop a sense of a bigger world beyond the setting;
- find out about what happens in the real world and interact directly with much more of its physical content, properties and behaviour;
- become aware of the people in their community, developing a sense of a bigger human world around them and of being part of that world;
- investigate and interrelate directly with the real world of humans – the range of people in the community, what they do, how they interact with each other, how they look after each other;
- use their bodies to negotiate space, play with environmental features for movement and being physical, and develop stamina and resilience over prolonged periods of activity;
- be with each other in different circumstances, interacting and developing relationships with other children and with adults;
- experience scale and perspective – up to huge and endless, and down to tiny and almost invisible;
- develop vision, especially in terms of a sense of space, distance, direction, height, spatial awareness, movement and learning to judge motion and speed;
- experience lots of strong stimuli for comments, questions and discussion, for natural conversation and for the growth of vocabulary, phrases and language in meaningful contexts;
- discover and examine a wide range of animals, plants and natural processes even in the most urban of settings;
- notice signs, symbols, numbers, letters and print in real contexts in the environment and develop understandings of how these convey meaning;
- gather an enormous amount of sensation, information and experience of the real world with which to explore and process through play and other creative activity back in the setting.

Figure 7.2 Every journey stimulates comments, questions and discussion.

Preparing to go out beyond the setting

For further sound advice on this area, I recommend Jennie Lindon's book *Planning for the Early Years: The local community* (Practical Pre-School Press 2012).

Parental engagement

It is really important to engage parents in this aspect of your outdoor provision before you begin to make use of it. Talk with them about what they did as children and what these experiences will have done for them. Discuss how their child might benefit from this layer of provision within your setting and ensure that they understand just what it is that you are proposing for their child. In England, you will need written parental permission for children to take part in outings, but a single, general permission for the whole time the child attends your service should be sufficient (a separate consent form would be needed for special full-day trips). As in all aspects of your provision, they should however be constantly informed about what their child is doing and see specifically how these particular experiences are supporting their well-being, learning and development. Images shown daily on a digital screen can be an excellent starting point. The child's experiences in this community and locality are likely to connect into their family lives, with information about home activity informing what happens in your excursions, and experiences in your locality spilling over into the child's home life.

Benefit–risk management

Thorough benefit–risk assessment and management planning is critical preparation for harnessing this extra layer of outdoor provision. Familiarity with this environment is key to practitioners feeling comfortable in it, and comfort is key to having confidence about being in it with young children. Being prepared and ready to deal with any circumstances that might arise results in a relaxed and successful excursion. I therefore recommend a fully researched and well-prepared, written benefit–risk management document for the routes and environments you plan to visit with children. Although in England the safeguarding and welfare requirements no longer require all risk assessments to be in writing, 'providers must determine where it is helpful to make some written risk assessments in relation to specific issues, to inform staff practice, and to demonstrate how they are managing risks if asked by parents and/or carers or inspectors' (*Statutory Framework for the Early Years Foundation Stage*, 2012, 3.63), and this is an area where a written document would clearly be helpful and supportive, especially when developing this area of practice. Settings will only need to do this once for the general situation and areas routinely visited, with dynamic assessment being used to manage change and developments on a daily basis.

The first step in the new approach to benefit–risk management is to analyse and state the rationale for taking children out into the local area in general, and for this location in particular. Make a clear case for the value and benefits to children and establish why this is an important part of your mission, ethos and provision. Being clear about the rationale and benefits helps you to take a positive and enabling approach to risk management, where action is taken to ensure that the experience is available to the children in a sufficiently safe way. Get to know the locations and routes, consider what changes might happen over time and through the year, and what consequences these might have for you. Assess the hazards or risks that may arise for the children, and identify the steps to be taken to remove/minimise and manage those risks and hazards. Identify aspects of the environment that need to be checked on a regular basis and check the route before use with children each time to see if there is anything new or different to manage. You do not need to re-write the general benefit–risk assessment for minor changes, but it is important not to become complacent. On-going 'dynamic' risk assessment will also be required for the daily excursion as you take the journey with children (just as you do for all other parts of provision), but good preparation should prevent staff from feeling anxious and ensure a relaxed approach with children.

Before you visit with children, make sure all the staff are comfortable and confident in being there themselves and for going there with young children. Induct any new staff carefully and discuss all issues to ensure that everyone always feels competent – do not put anyone in an uncomfortable position; make sure they air any concerns whatsoever and are fully prepared on a daily basis.

The overall benefit–risk management document could also cover agreed policy and procedures on:

- communication with parents – the processes and arrangements for gaining informed consent, and on-going sharing and discussion;
- consideration of required adult-to-child ratios – beyond legal requirements or guidelines, any need for lower ratios will result from consideration of what is appropriate for the circumstances and gives confidence to the participating staff, in the light of knowledge about your children and your staff;
- arrangements for extra voluntary helpers, trainees and students, including robust induction and good familiarity with the route and environment, and clarity about your approach for supporting the children;
- clear contingency arrangements and instructions, with useful telephone numbers;
- first-aid arrangements, medication and treatment protocols;
- road safety procedures and shared approach to stranger danger issues;
- toileting arrangements and sensible hygiene procedures;
- advising your insurance provider about this routine part of your practice (if required) and how your risk management processes meet safeguarding and welfare requirements.

Review your benefit–risk process and procedures for using the local area at least annually. Be sure to include a full staff discussion, evaluating how well it works and whether it needs adjusting.

Clothing and footwear

A sure way to ruin a lovely winter walk is to have cold feet hurting inside rubber wellie boots! As well as paying attention to appropriate and adequate clothing for both children and adults, ensure that feet are always warm, dry and comfortable, and carry spares in case of situations arising. Since bodies warm up when active, layers of clothing are the best approach so that children do not overheat and become uncomfortable. Children can carry their own backpacks to keep discarded clothing, spares and equipment. Adults should also carry extra spares for unexpected conditions. Other than this, try not to clutter children up with clipboards, binoculars and other resources, keeping their hands and bodies free for feeling and moving.

Prepare the children

An essential element of good planning is to prepare the children well. As usual, involving the children in deciding the rules and boundaries that will be needed to keep everyone safe and happy is the most effective way of ensuring that they remember and keep to them. A useful reminder is 'we look with our eyes, listen with our ears and think with our head' (Jenny Lindon, *The Local Community*, 2012, p. 3). Rules need to be simple and few – use only those that help children to make the most of their excursions. While on the journey, make sure children can always see an adult, so they can return to you if they feel insecure or alarmed.

Resources to enable excursions into the locality

Backpacks for adults and children (child-sized backpacks from *Mindstretchers* and *Early Excellence*) – children quickly learn to carry their own resources and this should be encouraged

First-aid kit (from *Muddy Faces*) – checked and replenished routinely and frequently

Specific medicines or treatments (such as inhaler or epipen) for individual children – ensure every adult knows about medical issues and can respond appropriately

Working telephone(s) – check this every day before leaving!

Useful telephone numbers (such as direct link to immediate help in the setting and relevant emergency numbers)

Clear contingency arrangements and instructions

High-visibility vests (if desired) (from *Muddy Faces* and *Open Ends*) or high-visibility strips for each person

Walking rope for managing dangerous points, such as road crossings – *Mindstretchers* has a rope with handles for up to six people that links to a puppet horse's head

Fresh drinking water in flask with cups (take washable cups rather than throw-away plastic cups)

Back-up rain-gear (for sudden downpours)

Warm clothes (change of socks, pairs of gloves, woollen hats, sun hats, etc.) – depending on the weather/season

Digital camera for adult use, notepad or Dictaphone

Magnifiers, binoculars, telescope

Robust digital cameras (*TTS* has a range of children's cameras)

Dictaphone or other recording device for children's use (from *TTS*)

Clipboards and plenty of pencils or felt pens

Small basket(s) or buckets for foraging and collecting interesting things

Figure 7.3 Streets are full of strange and fascinating things and events.

What might children notice and be interested in?

The possibilities for what children might notice and be attracted to really do seem to be endless. Since young children are so alert, and this environment so rich in stimulation, their attention might be drawn to many, many things, on any scale from the mighty to the miniscule – things which adults have long since ceased to be aware of or consider worth paying attention to. The real pleasure for accompanying adults at this slowed-down pace is the opportunity to be reminded about how fascinating these things actually are, to allow themselves to look at things afresh from a new perspective and a different point of view, and to let themselves be drawn into the detail, complexity and depth that ordinary everyday objects and events so often hold – especially natural ones. Adults will need to try very hard to slow their own looking right down, take much longer to react to children's comments or actions, wait to appreciate what children have actually noticed and give a long pause (try counting to ten!) before leaping in with what they already know from a lifetime's experience in our daily world. Once a child has noticed something in their surroundings, they often want to experience it and respond to it with several senses – feeling and listening as well as looking, perhaps smelling, and certainly by handling and moving it if this is possible. The biggest response children have is the need to use their body, and actions frequently follow looking. Be prepared for children to jump up and down with excitement or pleasure, to walk on top of walls, to balance along the curb stones or jump between paving stones.

The following is a list of some of the things young children might find interesting and want to respond to in the local environment around an average early childhood setting, but this is by no means exhaustive!

Ants and other tiny creatures
Babies, teenagers, elderly people
Big and enormous
Bin men, street sweepers, road-cleaning vehicles
Bridges and overpasses
Builders and building sites, diggers and cranes
Cars, buses, trucks and so on
Clouds, sky and effects of the weather
Colour, shine and reflection, light and dark, shadows
Curbs, paving stones and lines in the pavement (trajectories)
Dogs, cats, horses, pigeons, birds, squirrels, etc.
Doorways, doorsteps, windows, garage doors (going through)
Environmental print on shops – what it is for and what it all means
Fire and police stations, hospitals, residential homes for the elderly
Gates – open and shut, different types, handle and locks (going through)
Gutters and drains (trajectories)
Holes and 'homes' for small creatures and tiny people (enclosure)

House numbers and other numbers and letters in the street

Lamp-posts, lights, zebra crossing lollipops and other poles and posts

Listening to the sounds, smelling the smells, feeling the textures and shapes

Litter and litter bins

Manhole covers, patterns, textures

Mapping out a journey – pathways and intersections (connection)

Plants, weeds, flowers, flower shops, hanging baskets, containers

Posting letters, letter boxes

Postman/woman delivering letters and parcels

Print on buses, vans, lorries and other vehicles

Railings, safety barriers

Road safety, zebra crossings, pelican crossings

Roadworks, holes in the ground, construction workers

Roof tops, chimneys and buildings

Shops – supermarket, local shop, fish shop, bakers, DIY, household supplies, etc.

Steps, slopes and going up and down (up and down, vertical trajectory)

Things that carry and transport – such as buses, passengers and trailers (transporting)

Things that turn and rotate (rotation)

Tiny and miniscule – such as moss growing on the top of brick walls

Traffic signs, road markings, traffic lights

Trees and their trunks and roots

Figure 7.4 Young children notice and are drawn to the miniscule side of life.

Tunnels, alleyways, passages between buildings and other places to be under, inside or go through (enclosure, going through)

Water in the environment, especially puddles, rivulets, mud, footprints and tyre tracks

What is underground?

Wheels, bicycles, motorbikes, tractors

Further afield – where else might you go?

The focus of this chapter is centrally on the area *just outside* the setting, so that it can be visited easily, simply and repeatedly, becoming a familiar 'third space' in your provision (indoors, outdoors and just beyond the garden). It is important to select places that are very much in reach of small children going by foot in small groups, and that give plenty of scope for going slowly. If getting to the destination takes over the purpose of the excursion, the value is lost, since it is precisely the street or path itself and the journey along it that holds the value for each child. That said, there may well be places very close to your setting or school that can be part of this layer of provision. Here are a few possibilities, but what would work for you would clearly depend on your location:

Allotments, community gardens

Beach, stream, nature area

Blackberry picking

City and town squares and gardens

Farms, city farms and farm animals, aquaria

Garden centre

Going on the bus, by tram, by tube

Interesting buildings, city/town/village centre or special places/features

Library

Memorial and water features in town square

Park, playing fields, public playground, pathways with wooded or natural borders

Picnics and eating out – garden centre cafés are great for children

Places of worship, cemetery (these are often full of nature)

Shopping – supermarket, local shops, fish shop, etc.

Specialist shops or services, such as a travel agent, post office, bank, hairdresser or optician

Trains and train/bus stations

Waterways, canals, rivers, locks, boats

Getting the most out of your local excursions

- This layer of outdoor provision is very much about the area just outside your setting, beyond the gate but no further than young children can easily reach and cover at a slow pace, stopping to look closely whenever something catches their interest or revisiting something they were previously fascinated by, and taking time to explore and share thoughts about each thing. Pausing to watch while events take place is also important. This very local focus will do more to connect children to the locality and community than hurrying to go further afield.

- If children are going to become able to really tune into the richness of these areas, it is critical that each child experiences frequent visits, taking the same route and returning to the same places, on many occasions, that are reasonably close together. As the journey and the things in it become familiar and more predictable, the child can relax and begin to attend to more and more of what is going on.

- Revisiting allows pattern and change to be noticed, as well as enabling the child to deepen their awareness of detail and their understanding of what is happening. They can see more, experience more and have more material to work with back in the setting, processing these real and direct experiences through role play, small-world play, drawing and so on. All of this constructs the relationship that will give a growing sense of belonging to this community and locality.

- Other than preparing well for the excursion so that everyone is comfortable, confident and safe, avoid structuring the walk or having much of a purpose. The purpose is simply being in this place and allowing children to focus upon whatever they find interesting – so just let it flow and find its own course.

- 'Slowliness' is a strong feature of the kind of practice that will get the most from local excursions, and this has been referred to several times through this chapter. The strongest role for adults will be to 'walk alongside', more often than leading or following (Robin Duckett, Sightlines Initiative 2009) – figuratively as well as literally – and to be *genuinely* curious with the children, finding out and learning with them: what Rosemary Roberts has called 'companiable learning' (*Wellbeing From Birth*, Sage 2010)

- Being on foot and walking is another important component of this provision (unless the child has mobility issues or other physical difficulties). Current medical concerns about the severe lack of physical activity and excess of sedentary activity in the lives of even young children in the UK have resulted in official guidelines of at least three hours of physical activity a day (taken across the day and led by the child) and a reduction in the length of time children are sedentary (*Start Active: Stay Active*, Department of Health 2011). If our children are to lead healthy lives, we must get children out of containers and carriers as much as possible, and help to build fitness, stamina and robustness.

- Walking and being alongside will result in lots of conversation that flows naturally from both moving together and sharing what you are each noticing. Avoid filling the spaces between children's comments, giving time for them to think, make connections with their family lives and experience the desire to share these with you. You are likely to get to know a great deal about their relatives and pets, events in their lives and how they feel about things. You will almost certainly witness imaginative, creative, linguistic, logical, physical, emotional and social competencies that you had not realised before!

- Imaginative scenarios that emerge during one journey may well be picked up by other children and/or continue over into subsequent trips. Listen carefully to what these stories have to tell you about children's thoughts, concerns and fears, and developing capacity to make sense and meaning of their world (*37 Shadows* is a good example of this – see resources list at the end of this chapter).

- This layer of outdoor provision is a very three-dimensional environment. Pay attention to the ground below (and any opportunities to look beneath) and the leaf canopy, rooftops and birds above – and the sky beyond that. On some walks, take cameras with you and suggest to children that they photograph the things that interest them. Discussion at the computer back in the setting will reveal much more of what they have been attending to and why.

- The locality will also provide a very rich source of stimuli and material for children to investigate their persistent fascinations (schematic enquiries) and is filled with opportunities to explore transporting, trajectories, up and down, enclosure, boundaries and going through boundaries, rotation, connection and many other such big ideas. Knowing what children's specific on-going enquiries (schemas) are will help you to understand why they are especially interested in something along the way, and why they need to respond in this particular way. In the list above (in the section 'What might children notice and be interested in?'), I have highlighted some of the schema-related ideas that children might pick up on in the local environment.

- As well as walking or running, make the most of any physical features in the environment that encourage movement and action – walking along the tops of low walls and jumping off them, balancing along curb edges, leaping over paving stones. Squares and gardens in city and town centres tend to have lots of great features that children will easily find ways to use for physical activity.

- Play games too, such as funny walking and avoiding cracks in the pavement, and sing marching songs, such as The Grand Old Duke of York or The Wheels on the Bus. Try making sounds with the environment, such as running a stick fast and slow along some railings. Being the 'leader' for sections of the walk (knowing and showing the way) can give a child a great sense of competence and responsibility, and help them to map out the route in their minds.

- Children are natural foragers and hoarders, so hunting for and collecting special objects or 'treasure' will be very appealing. Although this might not feature in every trip, it is worth equipping children with small baskets or buckets on excursions when this is wanted, or when purposeful collecting is

Figure 7.5 Slow right down to absorb all the detail that children find so fascinating.

needed for a specific project back in the setting – and to always carry a collecting bag in the adult's backpack. An on-going display or nature table will be valuable – or even better perhaps, slowly build up a wall display of the route, mapping it out with the children and adding children's comments, questions, drawings and photographs.

The boundaries of the setting – letting the outside in

As well as going out into the local area around the nursery or school, there is much to be gained by thinking about how this world can be *brought into* the outdoor spaces within the setting. What is important is that children experience a sense of connectedness to the community they and their setting is part of. They need to be able to see into this world every day while they are exploring and playing outside, and aspects of this world need to be able to come into the outdoor environment, providing stimuli and material for children's own play. Very open boundaries around an outdoor area can result in the environment feeling too open and in children (and adults) feeling exposed, insecure, often somewhat windswept and sometimes rather caged. So to a large extent it is beneficial to enclose the outdoor environment with outer boundaries that are reasonably solid, providing emotional as well as physical protection. However, in doing this, it is important not to isolate the environment or children from the community and locality. A great way to enable this is to create ways for children to look into the area beyond through leaving some areas open, so that passing people and animals are noticed and responded to; constructing some lookout posts and places, so that children can choose to look out or down at the world beyond the boundary; having peep-holes at the right height for children, or even a periscope or (preferably) two. At Hind Leys Preschool, very high and solid fences surround the outdoor environment, but children can climb to the top of ladders safely placed side-by-side against them and chat together about what they see from this wonderfully empowering position up high. So valuable has this proved to be that, when a child was waiting for a turn at the base of the two ladders, the teacher realised that they needed another ladder so that she could join the other two children at the top.

If you have an open boundary or lower fence where people from the community (and their pets) pass by, consider how to balance making the most of this with fears of stranger danger. Children must grow up feeling secure in their community and able to get help when they need it.

It is also possible to make many connections to the local area and its community by bringing artefacts into the outdoor space or inviting parents to make items that become features to stimulate play in the environment. In an early childhood centre in Stockholm, Sweden, I saw an old moped half buried into the ground and many horse-like structures made by inventive parents out of wooden workhorses with brooms for the mane; in a centre in Melbourne, Australia, an old fireplace surround had transformed the sand pit into an inviting food-making area.

Figure 7.6 Children need to connect with the locality and community beyond the fence.

A seasonal outdoor alphabet

Over the course of many visits into your locality and community, and as a collaboration between children, parents and all the staff, gather good words related to the experiences, sensations and emotions of the season – through noting down words as they come up during the actual walks (children will be very drawn to a large notebook specially made for this purpose) and perhaps also on a 'seasonal alphabet wall' outdoors. This collection will bring greater awareness of just how many opportunities being in this special outdoor place holds, will focus attention on what children are really intrigued by in this fabulous 'extra' layer of outdoor provision and is likely to spark children's and adult's thoughts for planning both indoors and outdoors in the setting. As an example, here is an alphabet of feelings, things and activities for outdoors in winter:

An outdoor alphabet for winter

A – adventure, active, action...
B – bare earth, bare trees, branches, birds, blanket,
    burrow, black, brown, buds, bulbs, beacon...
C – candle, cosy, cave, cold, coats...
D – dark, damp, decorate...
E – evergreen, earth...
F – firelight, frost, fog, flocking, footprints, fallow, freezing/melting...
G – gloves, grey, ground, garlands...
H – home, hibernation, hats, holes...
I – ice, icicles, igloo...
J – jump, junctions...
K – kick...
L – lights, lantern, lamps...
M – mud, mixing, mud-pies, moon...
N – nesting, night...
O – owl...
P – puddles, pattern...
Q – questions, quiet...
R – rain, roosting...
S – sunset, sparkle, stars, sticks and stones, squelch, sky, snow, snowdrops, storm,
    surfaces, skeletons, shapes, scarves...
T – torch, texture, tracks...
U – underground, uncovered...
V – velvet, vapour trails...
W – warm, wood, waves, white, wet, waiting, wreath...
X – crossing – junctions, connections...
Y – yawn...
Z – sleep...

> *If a child is to keep alive his inborn sense of wonder ... he needs the companionship of at least one adult who can share it, rediscovering with him the joy, excitement and mystery of the world we live in.*
>
> (Rachel Carson, *The Sense of Wonder*, 1998)

Children's books to support experiences beyond the garden

After the Storm (and other Percy the Park Keeper stories) Nick Butterworth (Picture Lions 2003)

A Hole in the Road Jakki Wood (Frances Lincoln Children's Books 2009)

A Pig with Six Legs and Other Clouds: From the cloud appreciation society Gavin Pretor-Pinney (Sceptre 2007)

A Walk by the River Sally Hewitt (Franklin Watts 2005)

A Walk in the City (Little Nippers: Nature detectives) Jo Waters (Heinemann Library 2007)

A Walk in the Park (Little Nippers: Nature detectives) Jo Waters (Heinemann Library 2007)

Belonging Jeannie Baker (Walker Books 2008)

Bumper to Bumper Jakki Wood (Frances Lincoln Children's Books 1997)

Clouds That Look Like Things: From the cloud appreciation society Gavin Pretor-Pinney (Sceptre 2012)

Days Like This Simon James (Walker Books 1999) – collection of lovely short poems

Doors Alexandra Bonfante-Warren (Freidman/Fairfax Publishing 1998)

Exactly the Opposite Tana Hoban (William Morrow 1998) – photographs of opposites in everyday life

Half a World Away Libby Gleeson and Freya Blackwood (Scholastic 2012)

Having a Picnic Sarah Garland (Francis Lincoln Children's Books 2009)

Home Jeannie Baker (Greenwillow Books 2004)

In the Town: A picture word book Benedict Blathwayt (OUP Oxford 2007)

Listen, Listen Phillis Gershator and Alison Jay (Barefoot Books 2007)

Look, Look, Look Again: Winter, Spring, Summer, Autumn Claire Warden and Niki Buchan (Mindstretchers 2007)

Look Up, Look Down Tana Hoban (Greenwillow Books 1992)

Mummy's Magical Handbag Paulette Bogan (Bloomsbury Publishing 2005)

My Granny Went to Market: A round-the-world counting game Stella Blackstone and Christopher Corr (Barefoot Books 2006)

My Map Book Sara Fanelli (HarperCollins Children's Books 1995)

Out and About (Olly and Me) Shirley Hughes (Walker Books 1998)

Owen and the Mountain Malachy Doyle and Giles Greenfield (Bloomsbury Publishing 2001)

Shadows and Reflections Tana Hoban (Greenwillow Books 1990) – fabulous photographs from the street and daily outdoor life

Sheep Take a Hike Nancy Shaw and Margot Apple (Houghton Mifflin Company 1997)

The Dog Who Could Dig Jonathan Long and Korky Paul (OUP Oxford 2008)

The Green Line: A walk in the park Polly Farquharson (Frances Lincoln Children's Books 2011)

The Hill and the Rock David McKee (Andersen Press 2011)

The Listening Walk Paul Showers and Aliki (HarperCollins 1993)

★*The Once Upon A Time Map Book* B.G. Hennessy and Peter Joyce (Candlewick Press 1999)

The Wild Woods Simon James (Walker Books 2008)

★*Voices In The Park* Anthony Browne (Corgi Children's Books 1999)

Where My Wellies Take Me Clare and Michael Morpugo and Olivia Lomnenech Gill (Templar Publishing 2012)

Calendars come in a very wide range of subjects that will support children's interests, such as Britain from the air through to tractors and classic motorbikes – cut the pictures out and laminate them for outdoor use. Available from many suppliers, such as www. thegiftedstationeryco.com (located under 'Square Wall Calendars')

Catalogues with images of conservatories, gates, doors, windows and so on

Google Earth and Google Maps – give images at a huge range of scales

Magazines about the countryside, travel, vehicles, etc. – look for plenty of good colour images

Magazines with houses, buildings and DIY focusing on windows, doors, locks, etc. – look for plenty of good colour images

Maps of a range of scales and types, especially road maps

Further information and resources – specific guides to using your locality

Planning Educational Visits for the Early Years Anna Salaman and Suzy Tutchell (Paul Chapman Publishing 2005) – focuses on specific places such as galleries, museums, farms and so on, but a very useful section on the built environment

Planning for the Early Years: The local community Jennie Lindon (Practical Pre-School Press 2012) – a really excellent resource and recommended reading for this aspect of outdoor provision

Risk, Challenge and Adventure in the Early Years Kathryn Solly (Routledge 2013)

Walks and Visits (Key issues series) Dawn Roper (Featherstone Education 2009)

Further information and resources – useful books and resources

37 Shadows: Listening to children's stories from the woods – lovely analysis of the stories of three- and four-year-olds visiting their local woods over several weeks by Deb Wilenski (Cambridge Curiosity and Imagination 2012), from www.cambridgecandi.org.uk/shop

Adventures in Nature Building better childhoods: international perspectives series (Children in Scotland 2008)

Bridges (Our Earth Collection) Parkstone Press (e-Parkstone International 2010)

Developing a Forest School in Early Years Provision Jenny Doyle and Katherine Milchem (Practical Pre-School Books 2012)

Doing the Right Thing: Working with children in a natural environment, early childhood educators revalue their theory and practice DVD from Sightlines Initiative, www.sightlines-initiative.com (online store)

Doors Bob Wilcox (Firefly Books 2009) – a beautiful and extensive collection of colour photographs of doors around the world

Doors of the World Dominique and Jean-Phillip Lenclos (W.W. Norton 2005)

Forest Schools and Outdoor Learning in the Early Years Sara Knight (Sage Publications 2009)

I Love My World: Mentoring play in nature, for our sustainable future Chris Holland (2nd edition, Wholeland Press 2012)

Love Parks Week (annual event held at the end of July celebrating parks and green spaces) – offers a park health-check to post a review of your local park, www.loveparksweek.org.uk

Making the Most of Outdoor Learning Linda Thornton and Pat Brunton (Featherstone Education 2011)

Managing Risk in Play Provision: Implementation guide David Ball, Tim Gill and Bernard Spiegal (Play England 2008), available to download from www.playengland.org.uk (under 'Resources', then 'Managing Risk in Play Provision')

The Early Years Curriculum: A view from outdoors Gloria Callaway (David Fulton 2005)

The Great Outdoors: Restoring children's right to play outside Mary S. Rivkin (2nd edition, National Association for the Education of Young Children 2013)

The Little Book of All Through the Year Lorraine Frankish and Jan Stringer (Featherstone Education 2007)

The Little Book of Maps and Plans Marian Taylor and Melanie Roan (Featherstone Education 2012)

The Little Book of Outside in All Weathers Sally Featherstone (Featherstone Education 2003)

The Little Book of the Seasons Pat Brunton and Linda Thornton (Featherstone Education 2005)

The Sense of Wonder Rachel Carson, photographs by Nick Kelsh (HarperCollins Publishers 1998)

The Wild Weather Book: Loads of things to do outdoors in rain, wind and snow Fiona Danks and Jo Schofield (Frances Lincoln 2013)

Too Safe For Their Own Good? Helping children learn about risk and lifeskills Jennie Lindon (2nd edition, National Children's Bureau 2011)

Trail of Imagination and Curiosity – illustrated booklet created by CCI practitioners Filipa Pereira-Stubbs and Deb Wilenski, inviting families to playfully explore a Cambridge cemetery using their imagination and curiosity, from www.cambridgecandi.org.uk/shop

Windows of the World Jean-Philippe and Dominique Lenclos (W.W. Norton & Co. 2005)

Wingate Woodland School DVD package – film showing how Wingate Nursery School and Children's Centre has added another layer to their outdoor provision, available from www.wingatenursery.com (located under 'Training Base', then 'DVD Packages')

Young Children Talking: The art of conversation and why children need to chatter Di Chilvers (British Association for Early Childhood Education 2006)

Further information and resources – organisations and websites

Beach School and Forest School training – for information, contact The Forest School Association, currently hosted by the Institute for Outdoor Learning, www.outdoor-learning.org

Cameras – TTS educational suppliers has a VTech Kidizoom video camera, Tuff-Cam2 child-friendly digital camera and movie camera, and Easy-Speak MP3 recorder/player, www.tts-group.co.uk (located under 'ICT for Early Years')

Campaign for Learning Outside the Classroom (CLOtC) – has two early years teaching resource packs, www.lotc.org.uk (located under 'Resources/LOtC Resource Packs')

Federation of City Farms and Community Gardens – 120 city and school farms and nearly 1,000 community gardens up and down the country, www.farmgarden.org.uk

Health and Safety Executive – published a high-level statement in September 2012, *Children's Play and Leisure – Promoting a balanced approach*, which sets out the new official and legal position on striking the right balance between risk and benefit in providing play and learning experiences for children, www.hse.gov.uk/entertainment/childrens-play-july-2012.pdf

Living Streets – a charity campaigning to support the improvement and use of local streets and runs the Walk to School campaign, www.livingstreets.org.uk

Open Farm Sunday – annual event held in early June in which farmers across the UK open up their farms to the public, www.farmsunday.org/ofs12b/home.eb

Play Map – as part of their 'Exploring Nature Play' work, Play England have developed an interactive *Play Map* to help families and settings find good places for children to play and engage with nature across England. Visitors can add places, rate them and upload comments and images, www.playengland.org.uk/nature-play-map.aspx

The Woodland Trust has three very useful web pages – Nature Detectives club with free downloadable activities, www.naturedetectives.org.uk/club; seasonal outdoor play guides from www.naturedetectives.org.uk/schools (under 'Forest Schools Pack'); and free tree and seed packs for schools (short hedge and small copse packs) from www.woodlandtrust.org.uk/hedge

Visit Woods – the Woodland Trust also has a growing database of thousands of publically accessible woods that is searchable by postcode or place name and contains reviews and comments posted by visitors; a really useful resource that you can add to for other early years users, www.visitwoods.org.uk

Summary

- The streets and places just outside your early years centre are full of superb experiences that simply cannot be provided either indoors or outdoors in a setting or school.

- The spaces, places, routes, people, objects, actions and events in this locality offer an enormous range of possibilities with great potential for rich and meaningful experience, development and learning.

- The immediate locality just beyond your boundaries should be thought of as an additional layer of outdoor provision and a third environment in your provision (indoors, garden and just beyond).

- This locality should be very frequently visited, with very small groups, over a long period of time. This will build up comfort and familiarity, enabling children to dig deeply into what it has to offer them, connecting them to the place and its community, and giving a sense of belonging to a bigger world.

- Being prepared is key to success. All adults must be comfortable, confident, relaxed and able to handle any situations arising, and this is most effectively achieved through thorough and positive benefit–risk management processes.

- It is also very important to ensure that all parents are fully engaged beforehand with what it is that you are proposing for their child and are continually informed about what their child is doing and how these particular experiences are supporting their well-being, learning and development.
- As much as possible, children should be on foot and walking, so that they can interact fully with the many opportunities available. It is best to not go far so that it is not necessary to hurry, but aim also to gradually build up stamina and robustness over time.
- Excursions need to be at a slow pace, unhurried and on the child's agenda. It is important for accompanying adults to be able to stop and pay attention to children's interests – the goal is simply the journey itself and all the rich experiences it has within it. 'Slowliness' is a key pedagogical strategy. Other than being well prepared for safety and comfort, minimal structure and planning is recommended so that there is ample room to go with the flow.
- The adult's role is to walk alongside, learn 'companiably' with the children and allow themselves to be drawn into the detail, complexity and depth that ordinary everyday objects and events so often hold, especially natural ones.
- Ensure that there is plenty of opportunity for conversations. This is a wonderful way to get to know your children, and you are likely to discover aspects of their lives, families, interests and capabilities you were not previously aware of.
- Paying close attention during excursions, taking photographs and keeping notes on interests, interactions, experiences and events will enable these to feed into planning for indoor and outdoor provision in the setting, so that children can work on their rich first-hand experiences in play and other creative experiences.
- It is important that this layer of outdoor provision is well used all through the year, increasing the potential for learning through revisiting, repeating, witnessing change, making connections and uncovering the patterns in how things happen.

Index

Page numbers in **bold** denote colour figures.

Exploring Outdoor Play in the Early Years (Maynard/Waters) 7

Fancher, Lou 102, 129–30
fears and anxieties: and beyond the gate activities 170, 172; dealing with through construction/den play 137, 153
Featherstone, Sally 57, 133
feet 22, 31, 48, 53, 87–8, 91, 109, 114
Fitzenreiter, Valerie 36
flower pots 20, 118, 120, 125, 138
food 42, 63, 74, 172
foraging and gathering **52**, 73
Foreman, Michael 32, 57, 75, 129, 152
Forest School movement 139, 150
Foundation Phase (Wales) 2
Frederick (Lionni) 127
freedom 3, 9, 10, 16, 37, 82, 108, 137, 156
Froebel, Friedrich 139
further information and resources: beyond the garden gate 175–7; construction and den play 154–6; gardening and growing 77–8; the living world 77–9; for outdoor experience 12–14; physical play and movement 103–4; water play 33–4; wildlife 78, 79

gardening and growing **63**, **65**, **67**, **71**; children's books 75–6; construction/den play opportunities 139; container choice and positioning 64; equipment and resources 64, 67–9; further information and resources 77–8; links with home 62; opportunities offered by 63; plant selection 64, 67; tasks and decision-making 69–70; water play and 23, 31
Gardiner, Lindsey 102, 130
Garland, Sarah 31, 76, 101, 130, 174
gendered perspectives: construction and den play 150; creative and imaginative play 128–9; physical play and movement 90
girls 11, 90, 129, 150–1
gloop 28, 114
Goldsworthy, Andy 57, 131–2
Gonsalves, Rob 130
grass 42, 45, 49–50, 53, 90, 94, 111, 114–16, 122, 125, 137
gravel 37, 40, 42, 45, 49, 88–9, 92, 96, 118
guttering pipes 18, 23–4, 29–30, 43, 117, 140–1, 143

Haas, Eileen 136

hand-washing 53, 69, 109
Handa's Surprise (Brown) 74
Health and Safety Executive, website 7
health and safety issues: beyond the garden gate 159, 164, 167; construction and den play 139, 142; creative and imaginative play 120; leaf-play 42; the living world 68, 70, 74; mud play 47–8; natural materials 41, 42, 43, 46–8, 53, 139; physical play and movement 98–100; plants and seeds 42, 43; playing with feathers 43; responsibilities 7; sand play 46–7; soil 41; water play 25; wood 41, 139
Hewitt, Anita 22, 126
Hoban, Tana 56, 101, 174
Holmes, Oliver Wendell 136
Hughes, Shirley 32–3, 152–3, 174
Humphrey, Paul 57, 152
Hundertwasser, Freidensreich 129, 131
Hunter, Barbara 129

imaginative play, *see* creative and imaginative play
inclusion 7, 11
Inclusive Play (Casey) 7
Inkpen, Mick 32, 56, 76, 102, 153
Internet 6, 24, 53, 132
Isaacs, Susan 31

James, Simon 77, 174–5
Johnson, Steve 102, 129–30
Jung, C. J. 129

Kane, Barry 153
Kane, Tracy 57, 153
Kelsh, Nick 58
kitchen utensils 26, 48, 51, 94, 112

Lambert, Stephen 31, 76, 131
language development 21, 146
Learning through Landscapes 7, 57–8, 77
Lindon, Jennie 7, 162
Lionni, Leo 56, 75, 77, 127, 129
literacy 21, 124, 146
the living world **61**, **67**, **71**, **73**; activity suggestions 71–5; children's books 75–7; and dens/den play 42; health and safety issues 68, 70, 74; the importance of experiences with 60–2; information and resources 77–9; intimate contact with living things **68**; rhymes and songs 75; suitable settings 61–2, **65**;